NOT TO BE BROADCAST

A Da Capo Press Reprint Series

CIVIL LIBERTIES IN AMERICAN HISTORY

GENERAL EDITOR: LEONARD W. LEVY

Claremont Graduate School

NOT TO BE BROADCAST

BROADCAST

THE TRUTH ABOUT THE RADIO

By Ruth Brindze

DA CAPO PRESS • NEW YORK • 1974

Library of Congress Cataloging in Publication Data

Brindze, Ruth, 1903-
    Not to be broadcast.

    (Civil liberties in American history)
    Reprint of the ed. published by Vanguard Press, New
York.
    1. Radio broadcasting—United States. 2. Radio—
Law and legislation. 3. Radio broadcasting. I. Title.
II. Series.
HE8698.B66 1974   384.54'0973   73-19802
ISBN 0-306-70598-2

This Da Capo Press edition of *Not to be Broadcast* is an
unabridged republication of the first edition
published in New York in 1937.

Published by Da Capo Press, Inc.
A Subsidiary of Plenum Publishing Corporation
227 West 17th Street, New York, N.Y. 10011

Manufactured in the United States of America

NOT TO BE BROADCAST

NOT TO BE BROADCAST

THE TRUTH ABOUT
THE RADIO

BY

RUTH BRINDZE

AUTHOR OF

"HOW TO SPEND MONEY"

THE VANGUARD PRESS

NEW YORK

MANUFACTURED IN THE UNITED STATES OF
AMERICA BY H. WOLFF, NEW YORK

CONTENTS

NOT TO BE BROADCAST

I

MIGHTIER THAN THE SWORD

WHEN the Nazis attempted to seize power in Austria, their first move was not to murder Dollfuss, nor silence the press; they captured RAVAG, Vienna's chief radio station. When units of the Japanese army rebelled, their first move also was to seize the broadcasting station. Even before the bodies of the assassinated had stiffened, the killers were broadcasting their manifesto over the War Office Radio.

In Spain's Civil War the battles were fought with microphones as well as with machine guns, brickbats and daggers—the first real demonstration of the importance of radio in time of war. From the government-controlled stations there was a steady bombardment of propaganda against the rebels; from the radio stations seized by the rebels there was a heavy barrage of words against the government. The people of Spain and the world at large learned about the war only what the men controlling the radio facilities wished to tell them.

In war and in rebellion, fundamental facts stand out in sharper outline. The Nazis and the Japanese mutineers recognized that the party controlling the radio controls the nation; that radio is the key to the minds of the people; that public opinion is formed by the loudspeaker and that the masses are moved to action by a broadcast voice.

Dictators know this, and in the totalitarian states the radio is the propaganda instrument of the state. Rulers of other countries also know it.

When Franklin D. Roosevelt was campaigning for reëlection he was bitterly opposed by the press. He reached the people by radio. His landslide victory was a complete debacle for the publishers—a sensational ending of their monopoly of the manufacture of public opinion. On election day of the year 1936 the radio conclusively defeated and supplanted the press as America's No. 1 instrument for the control of the public mind.

Lesser politicians, demagogues, pleaders for special causes, good and bad, know the power of radio. The American Liberty League did not try to buy the press for their anti-New Deal propaganda; they sought to buy the facilities of the national networks. So also with The Crusaders. Father Coughlin would never have achieved any power in public affairs without the radio, nor is it probable that Huey Long would have enlisted thousands in his "Share the Wealth" society.

What is said in the press is still important; the freedom of the press must be jealously guarded. But freedom on the air is of still greater importance.

The question then is: Who should control the air waves, and how should they be controlled? In the totalitarian states the answer is easy; the government controls. In other European countries, whether they be democracies, quasi-democracies or dictatorships, the same is true; the government, directly or indirectly, rules the air waves. England, where freedom of the press has always been ardently defended, has made broadcasting a government monopoly, a branch of the post-office system.

In America, we have made it a private monopoly dominated by the government.

There are a few other countries where broadcasting is exploited for private profit—where audiences pay for entertainment by listening to descriptions of patent cures for constipation, itchy feet and pimples. But nowhere else in the world has the commercialization of radio been carried out on such a grand scale. The American system of broadcasting epitomizes America.

A people always crying "bust the trusts" has permitted a potent trust to gain control of the greatest instrument yet developed for propaganda and indoctrination.

The money changers, who were to be driven from the market place, sit as directors of our national and regional chains and of our "independent" stations and talk with the mighty voices of Morgan, Mellon and Rockefeller.

The power trust, whose shameless prostitution of the press and the schools is a matter of common knowledge and official record, has its representatives on the boards of directors and in the administrative branches of the broadcasting companies.

The medicine men and cosmetic manufacturers, notorious for making exaggerated—and sometimes dangerous—claims for their usuriously priced products, are the financial mainstays of radio stations.

Henry Ford and other industrialists are likewise good customers and can expect, and demand, that the broadcasters permit nothing to be said inimical to their interests.

Thus has America surrendered freedom of speech to Big Business.

As a check against the abuse of this tremendous power we have our old friend, the competitive system. One national network may refuse to broadcast a speech or an event; the other, either because its controlling interests are not affected or to curry favor, may accept the program. And even though both major networks turn thumbs down, there are always the smaller chains and the individual stations. Theoretically, competition assures freedom of speech on the air.

But in the paeans that are sung in praise of the American system of broadcasting, one pertinent fact is omitted. Broadcasting is controlled by our moguls of business and finance. This is the class which in Italy and Germany has benefited most from that new form of government known as

fascism. If fascism ever happens here, the new
leaders will not have to seize the radio; they already control it.

These are the men who now censor what the
vast radio audience may and may not hear; these
are the men who determine what economic theo-
ries may be expounded over the air, and what
ones may not. Aside from the pressure placed
upon them by their customers, the advertisers, it
is only natural that their editorial selections
should be determined by class interests.

Minority groups and individuals who have been
refused the privilege of broadcasting are continually charging censorship and discrimination.
And to whom do they turn to champion their
cause? To the government. Defenders of the
American system make much of the fiction that
broadcasting in the United States is free from
government interference or control. For this one
advantage alone, cry the broadcasters' apologists,
it is worthwhile to permit the exploitations of the
air waves—and the radio audience—for private
profit. The operators of radio stations know better. Only if they take orders from the Federal

Communications Commission may they engage in the broadcasting business.

The Radio Act of 1927, and the Communications Act which superseded it, explicitly denied the right of censorship to the federal authorities. Except for the prohibition against the broadcasting of obscene language, and the section requiring stations to grant equal privileges to all candidates for political office, operators of broadcasting stations were, by implication, to be free from any control or dictation by the government. Stations were to be licensed, and licenses were to be renewed when the public interest, convenience or necessity was served. But legal safeguards are open to broad interpretations. Although the letter of the law prohibits censorship, the interpretation of the law by the Commission, the courts, and the broadcasting companies has created a positive and growing censorship by the government. Exactly how this is carried on, we shall see in later chapters.

We shall also see how the power trust and all the vested interests censor and control what free men may hear. We shall see how gullibility is played upon, how public opinion is shaped by the money rulers of America.

Broadcasting is no longer an infant prodigy whose very achievement is a thing for marvel. It is already in its second decade of service— and disservice—to the American public. Admittedly, it is old enough to be judged. Let us investigate, then, how under the American system it has served the public interest, convenience and necessity.

II

THE AMERICAN WAY

NEWSPAPER readers may know that you can't believe everything you see in the papers; disillusioned gentlemen of the press may write of the suppression and coloring of news, yet even the cynics were shocked when an investigation of the utilities revealed positive proof of the ownership of newspapers by the power trust and the outright sale of news and editorial columns to the electric companies. But no fiery indignation has been aroused by the control of the radio by the electric industry, the bankers, and the big corporations. Here we have the most potent instrument devised by man for the forming of public opinion. And to whom have we entrusted it? To the money rulers of America.

The names of Morgan and Rockefeller are blazoned on the house flag of the National Broadcasting Company; the names of other bankers are woven into the pennant that flies from the masthead of the Columbia Broadcasting System. Lesser potentates of the business world—chambers of commerce, department stores, insurance companies—operate and dictate the policies of "independent" radio stations throughout the land.

This control by the vested interests is part and parcel of what we so sanctimoniously describe as the American system of broadcasting. It is a natural result of the public's shortsightedness during the broadcasting industry's first years.

The two great monopolies, the Bell Telephone System and the electric equipment manufacturers which developed broadcasting in America, had no longer vision. To the telephone company the new art of wireless communication appeared as a direct competitor of its wired system. As such, it had to be controlled. In 1923, the Bell System had formulated a plan for broadcasting patterned on its telephone monopoly. At an executive conference of telephone officials it was reported that:

"We have been very careful, up to the present time, not to state to the public in any way, through the press or in any of our talks, the idea that the Bell System desires to monopolize broadcasting; but the fact remains that it is a telephone job, that we are telephone people, that we can do it better than anyone else, and it seems to me that the clear, logical conclusion that must be reached is that, sooner or later, in one form or another, we have got to do the job."

For "leaders of the community—the chamber of commerce, the important newspapers, the department stores"—the report stated the telephone company would install radio transmitters. No one else might engage in the broadcasting business, for the telephone company controlled the patents to broadcasting equipment.

Behind this plan to monopolize broadcasting was no sinister attempt to control public opinion. The telephone company was primarily interested in continuing its monopoly of communication services; secondly in securing revenue from its patents.

The electric equipment manufacturers were also motivated by the profit impulse. The General Electric Company held fundamental patents for the construction of radio transmitters and receiving sets. The Westinghouse Electric and Manufacturing Company controlled other important patents. The patents of both of these companies, those owned by the Bell System and of several other companies, were pooled in the Radio Corporation of America.

General Electric and Westinghouse were to have the monopoly of the manufacture of radio receiving sets; the Bell System was to have the monopoly of broadcasting. Radio, and everything that pertained to it, was to be controlled by a trust.

Monopoly is not a fighting word—when the monopoly produces free entertainment. Radio "fans" of the 1920's were satisfied to have the electric and telephone companies run the show. Radio was a toy, a public nuisance, a gadget that induced "fans" to sit up all night, and after ear phones were supplanted by loudspeakers, that also disturbed their neighbors' rest. Radio was merely a new medium of entertainment. Who in those early days realized that the toy would become a weapon mightier than the sword?

The press was, from the first, recognized as a

molder of public opinion. Journalists established newspapers not only to report the news but also to interpret it. They boasted of their freedom. Broadcasting in America has no such history. It has always been a "kept" industry.

In the beginning, the electric companies were willing to supply free entertainment because the public would buy radio sets only if there were words and music on the air. The telephone company was willing to establish broadcasting stations to demonstrate to "leaders of the community" the desirability of leasing a station from the Bell interests. Later on, advertisers were willing to assume the burden of support because broadcast advertising increased sales. Broadcasting in America has always been an industry whose primary purpose has not been public service but private profit.

Except for the rigidity of the trust structure, the American system of broadcasting was permitted to develop without a plan. The telephone company owned station WEAF of New York, one of the most mechanically perfect of the pioneer stations. In 1922, the station's management decided that broadcasting was expensive, and that the public should not expect free entertainment. An appeal was made for contributions, and when the receipts proved disappointing, some genius of merchandising conceived the idea of selling "time" on the air. Thus was developed the commercialization of broadcasting.

Opera stars, actors from Broadway, attracted by the novelty of the new instrument and the opportunity for publicity, were glad to broadcast. Station WEAF had good program material available free. It also had telephone wires at its disposal. It was only natural, then, for someone to suggest that stations be linked by wires and that the New York programs be transmitted by wire to other stations. So the network system originated.

Under a law enacted in 1912 for the regulation of radio equipment on coastwise and transoceanic shipping, the government was authorized to license operators of radio transmitters. The purpose was to increase safety at sea by requiring ships to carry skilled operators. When popular broadcasting began, the owners of radio stations were also obliged to secure a license. So, entirely through chance, and without any conception of the long-time results, the government established its right to control the broadcasting industry.

Business expediency, the special interests of the telephone company, the application of an old law—these three were the determining factors in the development of the American system of broadcasting.

The telephone company withdrew from broadcasting in 1926. Station WEAF was sold to the Radio Corporation of America which organized a subsidiary, the National Broadcasting Company, to enter the broadcasting business. For another three years the Bell System continued to control the industry and to secure a revenue from broadcasting through its licensing system. Only stations which had purchased transmitters from the Western Electric Company, Bell's manufacturing unit, or which had been licensed by the telephone company, could secure from it the wires necessary for the transmission of wireless messages.

The stranglehold of the Radio Corporation of America over the manufacturers of receiving sets was theoretically ended by the consent decree of

1932 which terminated the government's action against the RCA for alleged violation of the anti-trust laws. The General Electric and Westinghouse companies were ordered to withdraw from the trust and the RCA was no longer to be the exclusive licenser under the patents of its former members; each company was to have the power of licensing under its own patents. The Radio Corporation, however, was to have a non-exclusive licensing privilege, and since radio patents interlock, "independent" manufacturers must still seek a permit from the RCA which alone has the power of licensing under all the patents.

Although the National Broadcasting Company was one of the defendants to the suit, the government made no effort to end the control of the broadcasting unit by the radio combine. Under the provisions of the Radio Act of 1926, the broadcasting licenses of National Broadcasting Company's stations might have been revoked. The licensing authority made no such move.

Long before, broadcasting had been recognized as an industry for the "big fellows." There never was enough room in the "broadcast band" for everyone who wished to broadcast. When assignments of frequencies were originally made, preference was given to the well-equipped stations of the National Broadcasting Company and to those of the electric companies and of other groups with strong financial support. The quality of the transmission equipment, not the character of the ownership, determined who should be assigned the best wave lengths.

The broadcast band originally included the frequencies between 550 and 1500 kilocycles. Less than one hundred of the frequencies could be assigned since radio waves collide and cause interference unless there is adequate separation between the frequencies on which stations operate. Each frequency, however, can be used by several stations, so located and constructed that the broadcasts of one do not interfere with those of another. Assignments to some of the frequencies were made in this way. But forty of the wave lengths were set aside as "clear channels" for the exclusive use of a single station after nightfall. The clear-channel assignments immediately created an aristocracy of the air—a favored few to whom special privileges were granted. These assignments were made to the powerful stations, those operated by the National Broadcasting Company and by similar interests which could afford to maintain high power transmitters.

Clear channels have never been fully utilized. It was necessary to await the development of sufficiently high-powered transmitters to overcome the natural interference hazards. It was also necessary to wait until the installation of such transmitters was financially sound, until the charges for their maintenance could be met by advertising revenue. There is now only one clear-channel station, WLW of Cincinnati, operating a 500,000-watt transmitter, ten times more powerful than any other in the country. This station reaches the radio audience in nineteen states. Many other stations are now ready to install equally powerful transmitters. In 1936, however, the government's licensing authority was hesitant to permit such increase of transmitting power because it would finally make broadcasting an activity in which only ultra-big business could engage. Whether the lobbyists for the clear-channel group will be successful in securing increased transmission power remains to be seen.

The clear-channel group has become more select than ever. Because of the demand for wave lengths, the original ruling on clear channels has been modified, and in many instances more than one station has been assigned to a frequency originally set aside for exclusive use. Only twelve channels now remain clear. These are held by six stations of the National Broadcasting Company, four of the Columbia Broadcasting System and three of the Mutual Broadcasting System.[1]

The maintenance of these clear channels is only one of the major concerns of the potent units of the broadcasting world. Assignments to the ultra-high frequencies, or the short waves, are soon to be made. A vast new empire of the air is to be divided, and the aristocracy of the air, the companies operated by and for Big Business, have put in their bids for preferred positions.

They claim special consideration for their applications because of the service their engineers have rendered in developing the use of the short waves. They ask that the "experimental licenses" granted for this development work be continued

[1] The total comes to thirteen because station WLW is a member of both the NBC and the Mutual systems.

as permanent grants. This is the practice that was followed in assigning wave lengths when the boundary of the broadcast band was moved from 1500 kilocycles to 1600 kilocycles. If it is applied to the assignment of the short waves, Big Business will be granted a complete monopoly over broadcasting—and the molding of public opinion in America.

For the short waves will bring us television— with its power to direct the mass mind hidden behind a movie appeal. It will mean more direct competition between broadcasting and the movies which "entertain" by projecting flickering pictures on a screen. But the short waves will also bring us facsimile. By special attachments, radio receiving sets in each home will be transformed into printing presses activated by master devices in key radio stations. When the cost of facsimile attachments is brought within the popular price range, and this is a possibility of the next few years, the public will be completely under the control of the men who operate radio stations. The press, as it exists today, will have an overpowering competitor. The distribution of news by facsimile will be immediate and direct. Within a few minutes after the occurrence of world events, printed reports and illustrations will issue from the radio receiving sets. Without cost, except perhaps that of paper and the initial expenditure for the machine, the American public will awake each morning to find its newspaper printed and ready on the radio.

This device will make an anachronism of even the most modern printing plants. Twenty-four hours a day the efficient radio press will produce a mass of printed words and vivid pictures— more than enough to supplant not only the newspapers but magazines and books. The circulation of this new medium will encompass the entire country and put to shame the present circulations of our popular newspapers and magazines.

The advent of television and facsimile is no dream. Both have reached almost mechanical perfection. Their introduction to the public has purposely been delayed for economic reasons. The monopolists who developed sound broadcasting intend to continue their control of radio in its extended fields of television and facsimile.

The threat of such domination by Big Business is too great—too immediate—to be overlooked.

The monopolistic American system of broadcasting developed before the power of radio was understood. Now that we know that the toy has become an instrument for control, it is time to take stock.

III

WHO OWNS THE AIR?

Who says there is a monopoly of broadcasting? The public relations directors of the national networks refute such a charge, but the advertising directors confirm it. This does not indicate inter-departmental confusion. Both viewpoints are correct but one is better fitted for the ears of the general public than the other.

There is a growing antipathy to bigness. Very well, then. The publicity department proclaims that the holdings of the National Broadcasting Company in the radio world are not big. The NBC owns only ten stations and operates five others. The number of stations owned and operated by the Columbia Broadcasting System is even less impressive; in all there are ten, eight owned and two operated under leases. The Mutual Broadcasting System, the third national network, is a coöperative enterprise and owns no stations.

Of the 685 radio stations in the United States then, the two major chains have absolute control over only 25. Even if the expert in syllogistic logic were to continue one step further and include in the arithmetical calculations all stations affiliated with the networks, the total would by no means be overwhelming. In the Blue and Red networks of the National Broadcasting Company there are 111, while in the Columbia System there are 99. In other words, only 29 percent of the radio stations in the country are members of either of the Big Two.[1]

But in the radio world it is not number but transmitting power and the desirability of the wave length that counts. The major networks and the Mutual System control every high-powered station in the country and every clear channel. Their stations are so strategically located that the network programs are transmitted from the Atlantic Coast to the Pacific, from Mexico into Canada. Of the 22,869,000 "radio homes" in the United States, the National Broadcasting Company estimates that it reaches approximately 22,500,000. The circulation claimed by

[1] These figures are as of January 1, 1937.

the Columbia network is even greater. According to the last United States Census, there were 4.1 persons in the average family. The circulation of each of the networks then has passed the hundred million mark. The combined daily circulation of all the newspapers in the country is estimated at 38,450,000. These are the figures emphasized by the advertising departments. For example, of its 50,000-watt clear-channel station WBT of Charlotte, North Carolina, the Columbia Broadcasting System advertises that it "sends its voice as far north as Canada!— There are 11 other stations in the Carolinas, but all of them put together cannot cover as much territory as WBT alone,—a territory which needs and supports 50 daily newspapers." [2]

The dominant position of the chains is most clearly illustrated by the power of their transmitting apparatus. The total transmission power of all broadcasting stations in the United States is 2,634,200 watts. This is divided among the networks and the independents in the following proportions:

[2] *Broadcasting,* 1936 Yearbook Number.

NBC Red & Blue Networks
(111 Stations)   1,686,100 watts
Columbia Broadcasting System
(99 Stations)   644,900   ''
Mutual Broadcasting System
(42 Stations)   690,200   ''
    Total controlled by the chains 2,447,600   '' [3]
    Total controlled by all others   186,600   ''

In other words, the stations that comprise the two major networks have 88.4 percent of the total transmitting power; the three networks have 92.9 percent. Only 7 percent is assigned to "independents" and to non-commercial stations.

Still another method of illustrating the domination of the industry by the chains is the share they take of the advertising revenue. In 1935, the total net advertising revenue for all broadcasting stations was $86,492,652. Of this sum, the networks took half—to be exact, 49.9 percent —for chain broadcasting. Of the remaining half, a substantial portion was pocketed by the same

[3] Because many stations are members both of Mutual and of one of the other major networks, in the total computation an allowance has been made for this duplication. The transmission power of both the NBC Networks and the Mutual System includes the 500,000-watt station WLW of Cincinnati.

TRANSMISSION POWER
OF ALL BROADCASTING
STATIONS

N. B. C.
RED & BLUE NETWORKS
111 Stations

ⱕⱕⱕⱕⱕⱕⱕⱡ

COLUMBIA
99 Stations

ⱕⱕⱕⅼ

MUTUAL
42 Stations

ⱕⱕⱕⱡ

ALL OTHERS

ⱕ

Each symbol represents 200,000 watts

stations that comprise the chains for commercial programs transmitted only over one of the affiliated stations.

The advertising contracts of both major chains require that, except under special circumstances, member stations must accept the network's commercial programs. The "sustaining programs" originated by the networks and used to fill in time which no advertiser has bought need not be broadcast by members of the chains. But they usually are. For a radio station licensed to operate on "full time" is on the air sixteen or more hours a day and the average station is glad to solve its problem of what to broadcast by using the majority of the networks' "sustaining" features. Thus the officials of the networks determine the radio entertainment of the nation. Broadcasting, as it is operated in the United States, is the networks' show.

THE NATIONAL BROADCASTING COMPANY

The National Broadcasting Company, wholly owned subsidiary of the Radio Corporation of America, controls the most powerful chain in the country. Its board of directors is chosen from the directorate of the RCA; its president is named by men who are directors of the broadcasting subsidiary as well as of the parent company. Although it is frequently asserted that the broadcasting unit is operated independently of the Radio Corporation, its management is directly responsible to the same men who direct the affairs of the radio trust. Who are these men and what interests do they represent? [4]

BOARD OF DIRECTORS OF THE RADIO CORPORATION
OF AMERICA

Chairman of the board is General James G. Harbord, a Morgan man. The retired general is also a director of Morgan's Bankers Trust Co. (which loaned $20,000 to the Liberty League), the Atchison, Topeka & Sante Fe Railroad, the New York Life Insurance Co. and American Legion Publishing Corporation.

[4] The small investor in RCA stock has no voice in the directorate. At the 1933 annual stockholders' meeting, for example, 72 percent of the voting was done through proxies, and the form of proxy supplied, according to Dr. W. M. W. Splawn, "was not designed to make it convenient to stockholders to exercise their right to appoint and constitute proxies other than those whose names appear thereon. . . ." In other words the proxies were designed to perpetuate the directorate and management. (Report on Communications Companies—House Report 1273.)

Newton D. Baker, legal adviser to Morgan utilities, prominent in Liberty League affairs, is a director of seven other companies including the Mutual Life Insurance Co., Cleveland Trust Co., Baltimore and Ohio Railroad and Goodyear Tire & Rubber Co.

Cornelius Bliss is a member of the investment firm of Bliss Fabyan & Co. and a director of the (Morgan) Bankers Trust Co.

The Mellon interests are represented by Arthur E. Braun of Pittsburgh, president of the Mellon-dominated Farmers Deposit National Bank (one of whose directors is A. W. Robertson, chairman of Westinghouse), of the Reliance Life Insurance Co. in which the Mellons are financially interested, and of the Suburban Rapid Transit Street Railway. He is also a director of Allegheny Steel Co., Harbison-Walker Refractories Co. (another of whose directors is Richard K. Mellon), and Duquesne Light Co., one of the utilities which comprise the Byllesby group, etc.

Next in alphabetical order is Bertram Cutler, described in Poor's *Register of Directors* as "with John D. Rockefeller." Cutler was elected to the board after the RCA's leases in Rockefeller

Center were adjusted by the issue to the Rocke-
fellers of 100,000 shares of stock.

John Hays Hammond, Jr., is president of
Radio Engineering Corporation and consulting
engineer both for RCA and its two former affili-
ates, General Electric and Westinghouse. He is
the inventor of torpedoes and other projectiles
controlled by wireless, an officer of the Crown
(Italy), an honor bestowed by Mussolini, and
the holder of more than six hundred patents on
radio, pipe organs, and military devices. He
licenses the RCA and the American Telephone
and Telegraph Company to use these patents
for commercial purposes only; the United States
government has the option of using them for
military purposes.

Edward J. Nally, a septuagenarian who
retired from active service in 1925, was taken
over by the RCA with the Marconi Wireless
Telephone Company of which he was then vice
president. He played an important rôle in the
early days.

Edward Harden, DeWitt Millhauser and
Frederick Strauss are representatives of the
brokerage houses and underwriters which have

helped to raise funds for the RCA. Harden, a brother-in-law of Frank Vanderlip, is a member of Baker, Weeks & Harden. He serves on the board of half a dozen RCA subsidiaries. Mill-hauser is a partner in Speyer & Co., underwriters of utility and railroad issues. Strauss represents J. & W. Seligman & Co., which helped to finance the RCA's purchase of the Victor Company.

James R. Sheffield, corporation lawyer, former president of the Union League Club and the National Republican Club, was elected to the board in October, 1927, shortly after his resignation as ambassador to Mexico. In its editorial on his appointment the *New York Times* wrote: "He is fluent in speech, with a pleasing presence and on ceremonial occasions will be a credit to his country." Sheffield was ambassador during the Obregon-de la Huerta régime, when the pressure exerted by American mining and oil interests almost forced armed intervention by the United States. In the early days of the RCA, when the trust was attempting to monopolize radio communication to the South American countries and China, Sheffield had been called upon to use his good graces with the State Department. While the Republicans were in office, Sheffield had important political connections.

David Sarnoff's rise to fame and fortune is on the Horatio Alger model except that his dominant position in the industry is due largely to his ability to negotiate with bankers. He is chairman of the board of the National Broadcasting Co.

Besides the financial affiliations of the Radio Corporation's directors, their personal sentiments on such important matters as war and peace are significant. For controlling as they do one of the largest networks in the country—and the world —they are in an almost unsurpassed position to mold the public mind. Newton D. Baker was, of course, President Wilson's Secretary of War. General Harbord is a retired army man who believes that:

"War represents a permanent factor in human life and a very noble one. It is the school of heroism from which a nation's noblest sons graduate into highest manhood. . . . Individual preparation for national defense is necessary for the peace-time benefits that come to the people who prepare themselves, for the efficiency that will come when your streets will again echo the tread of marching soldiers, your railways and your waterways again teem with men and implements of war assembling to protect the flag. . . ." [5]

Colonel Manton Davis, general attorney for the Radio Corporation, testified at a congressional hearing that the trust is "an organization whose every important official and technician is a reserve officer of the army or navy." John Hays Hammond, Jr., although not a munitions manufacturer, is, because of his inventions, closely allied to the murder-for-profit industry. Altogether, a jingoistic crew to entrust with the control of public opinion.

In the autumn of 1936, Messrs. Sarnoff, Baker, Bliss, Harden, Millhauser, Sheffield, Strauss and Lenox R. Lohr were the directors of the National Broadcasting Company. Major Lohr, who succeeded Merlin H. Aylesworth as president of the NBC, came to his new post from the army via the Chicago World's Fair. He had had no experience in broadcasting but so impressed were the directors with his successful management of the Fair that they chose him to head the network. Under his aggressive leader-

[5] Speech quoted by Raymond B. Fosdick in *The Old Savage in the New Civilization.*

ship the chain has rapidly increased its sphere of influence.

His fundamental policies do not appear to be different from those established by Aylesworth during the ten years that he was president of the company. Testifying before the Federal Communications Commission in October, 1936, Major Lohr spoke at length of the many public services rendered gratis by his company, of its broadcasting of public events, educational programs, and so on. Then in a forthright manner he declared: "We would not have you believe that NBC's concern for the radio audience is one of pure altruism . . . in the long run, he who serves best profits most. . . ."

Some years before, Mr. Aylesworth had also declared that there was "no altruism" in the policies of the NBC and that the broadcasting of such programs as those sponsored by the Foreign Policy Association, the Federal Council of Churches, and the National League of Women Voters were "good advertising."

The sensitivity of the NBC to public opinion was not so great in those days as it is at present. Before Mr. Aylesworth's appointment as presi-

dent of the network, he had been managing director of the National Electric Light Association.
While he was directing the affairs of the National
Broadcasting Company, the Federal Trade Commission was conducting its investigation of the
public utilities and in its report published the
following letter to indicate the propaganda methods employed by the former manager of the Light
Association. Aylesworth had written:

"I would advise any manager who lives in a community where there is a college to get the professor of
economics interested in your problems. Have him lecture
on your subject to his classes. Once in a while it would
pay you to take such men, getting $500 or $600 a year,
or $1000 perhaps, and give them a retainer of $100 or
$200 a year for the privilege of letting you study and
consult with them. For how in heaven's name can we
do anything in the schools of this country with the
young people growing up if we have not first sold the
idea of education to the college professors?"

The directors of the NBC did not consider this,
nor other disclosures, sufficient reason for reliev-
ing Mr. Aylesworth of his post in the broadcasting industry.

The testimony before the Senate's Banking

and Currency Committee in 1933 shows that Mr. Aylesworth continued the practice of buying professorial prestige at bargain rates after he went into the broadcasting business. At his suggestion the investment banking firm of Halsey, Stuart & Company, underwriters of Insull securities, retained Professor Nelson of the University of Chicago to act as its mouthpiece on the air. When Mr. Stuart was being examined, the senators were inquisitive about the radio program.

SEN. REYNOLDS: What was the name of the "Old Counsellor"? What was his name?

MR. STUART: I ought to remember it. He is a professor of note at the University of Chicago.

SEN. REYNOLDS: At the University of Chicago?

MR. STUART: Yes, sir.

SEN. REYNOLDS: How much did you pay him per week?

MR. STUART: $50 a week. I will remember it later. It was Nelson.

SEN. REYNOLDS: Professor Nelson?

MR. STUART: Yes, sir.

SEN. REYNOLDS: Is he still at the university?

MR. STUART: I think so. Of course, everything he delivered was written for him. He was simply the deliverer of it.

SEN. REYNOLDS: Who wrote it?

MR. STUART: It was written in our office.[6]

Aylesworth was "kicked upstairs" in 1936, becoming vice-chairman of the NBC, an advisory post for which he received only $10,000 a year. The balance of his annual wages was paid by Radio-Keith-Orpheum, a corporation in which RCA was financially interested and which Aylesworth served first as president, then as chairman of the board. But this arrangement did not last long. Eight months after he had become special adviser to NBC, Aylesworth resigned and it was announced that he would devote all his time to the movie-vaudeville company. A few months thereafter, when Floyd Odlum of the Atlas Corporation and Lehman Brothers had bought control of RKO and their plan of "reorganiza-

[6] Aylesworth gave an entirely different version of the Old Counsellor program when he appeared before a House Committee on Jan. 24, 1929. Then he said: "So we organized a program of music and we created a character called the Old Counsellor. Frankly I will tell you that he was an actor and we chose him because of his voice and not because of his banking intelligence. We prepared his speech copy so people would listen to it, and Halsey-Stuart, when they heard of it, said that it was a wonderful thing. They did not know whether they would get a nickel out of it, they said, but they would sponsor it and we must make the program. We did. . . ."

tion" was before the court, the bankers' own man was running their show business and Aylesworth was again eased out.

Probably the Radio Corporation could have found another job with still another of its subsidiaries for the man who had developed for it the biggest network in the world. But Mr. Aylesworth is not one to be crowded from pillar to post. He washed his hands of RCA and took a job with the Scripps-Howard newspapers.

His qualifications for a top-notch position with the liberal, anti-public utility, Scripps-Howard newspapers is a matter of public record. He knows the newspaper business as only a propagandist for the special interests can know it.

But although he touchingly declared that he had long entertained "the ambition to enter the publishing field," it is doubtful if Mr. Aylesworth's special talents will be applied to the newspaper business. Scripps-Howard has also long entertained radio ambitions—to build a radio chain comparable to its newspaper holdings—and here is where Mr. Aylesworth's experience will prove most useful. According to the mellifluous Owen D. Young, "It was Mr. Aylesworth's ingenuity and adaptability amounting in fact to positive genius which blazed the new trail of broadcasting in this country and set the pace which others have followed." He now has another opportunity to use to good advantage the experience he gained during twenty-odd years of service to the electric industry.

The National Broadcasting Company itself has outgrown the original purpose for which it was organized by the electric manufacturers who established the radio trust. Today, the NBC is far more than a fountain supplying free entertainment to stimulate the sale of General Electric and Westinghouse radio sets. In 1935 it accounted for approximately one-third of the Radio Corporation's total gross income.

With the independents threatening the Radio Corporation's supremacy in the manufacture and sale of radio receiving sets, it is becoming apparent that the broadcasting unit may soon be the corporation's most valuable property. The NBC is now severely handicapped by its relationship to the trust; even though its spokesmen take every opportunity to declare that the broadcasting subsidiary is interested only in broadcasting, it still bears the stigma of the mother company. If this burden increases in weight at the same rate as it has been in recent years, it is not unlikely that the bankers who control the company may find it expedient to grant the broadcasting unit a financial divorce.

At the hearings before the Federal Communications Commission in June, 1936, preparatory to assignment of wave lengths in the ultra-high frequencies, many unkind remarks were made about the monopolistic practices of the RCA. An interesting result of one of these attacks was the hiring of Oswald F. Schuette to act in an advisory capacity to the Radio Corporation. For many years, Schuette had been one of the most active and vociferous representatives of the independents, and at congressional hearings and other investigations had testified to the monopolistic control of the Radio Corporation of America. Now his services have been bought by the RCA.

Although Schuette was silenced, Samuel E. Darby, Jr., representing eleven of the largest independent manufacturers of radio receiving[7]

[7] American Bosch, Philco, Zenith, Crosley, Sears Roebuck, Montgomery Ward, Emerson, Stromberg Carlson, Motorola, Stewart Warner, Spartan.

sets, achieved wide publicity for his remarks when Boake Carter, Philco's popular news commentator, repeated them almost in their entirety over the Columbia network. Philco, it should be noted, is one of the licensees of the Radio Corporation which has frequently chafed under the trust's yoke. As a result of the Carter broadcast, it is reported that David Sarnoff paid a visit to his rival, William Paley, president of the Columbia Broadcasting System, to remonstrate for permitting the broadcasting of the derogatory statements. Counsel for the Radio Corporation was also reported to have scanned a transcript of the Carter remarks "with a view to finding whether it contained anything that might be considered libelous to the radio combine." Apparently there was no legal cause for action. The publicity, however, did the RCA no good, and the recurring rumors that Congress will move for another investigation of the radio trust is making the directors of the Radio Corporation decidedly apprehensive. As consolation, they can remember that the trust has been officially investigated many times in the past, that it has withstood the sniping of the little fellows, and has always come out on top. With its control of many important patents for television and facsimile broadcasting, the RCA has every prospect of continuing to dominate the radio industry.

THE COLUMBIA BROADCASTING SYSTEM

Unlike its competitor, the Columbia Broadcasting System is not owned by nor affiliated with any manufacturer of radio equipment. Since 1932, when it bought back the 50 percent interest in the network which had been sold to Paramount-Famous Players Lasky Corporation four years before, the Columbia Broadcasting System has been controlled by the Paley family and the bankers who supplied the cash needed to repurchase the stock from Paramount.

Columbia stock is not listed on any Exchange, and although there is some trading in it in over-the-counter transactions, comparatively little of it is held by the general public.

When the network was founded in 1927 as the United Independent Broadcasters, Inc., the captains of the electrical equipment business who were steadily losing money on the National

Broadcasting Company were tremendously amused at the idea of anyone contemplating a profit from broadcasting. At first it seemed as though they were right. The founders of the new organization—Major J. Andrew White, one of the old-timers of commercial broadcasting and formerly a vice president of the RCA subsidiary, Wireless Press, Inc., Arthur Judson, manager of concert stars, and George A. Coats, a promoter—were soon in a bad hole. Coats had gone on the road to build a chain, and had signed up sixteen stations by guaranteeing to buy ten hours a week from them at $50 per hour. The resulting total of $8,000 weekly was, in those days, a staggering sum for any network. In the nick of time, a good angel appeared in the form of the Columbia Phonograph Co. which bought the operating rights of United Independents, because it was worried by the premature announcement that its rival, the Victor Talking Machine Co., was about to be gathered in by the acquisitive Mr. Sarnoff. But after three months of broadcasting at a loss, reputed to have been $100,000 a month, the phonograph company was ready to retire. United Independent bought back the operating company, then known as the Columbia Phonograph Broadcasting System, for $10,000.

Dr. Leon Levy, a former dentist, and the owner of WCAU, one of the stations which had been signed up by Coats, produced the next angel, Jerome H. Louchheim, friend of the late W. W. Atterbury and, according to *Fortune,* "other big shots in Quaker Town." Soon the Columbia Broadcasting System had a reported $150,000 of Louchheim's cash in its treasury, and its affiliated stations had been persuaded to sign a new contract releasing the network from the weekly guarantees. This contract is one of the reasons for the success of the Columbia Broadcasting System. Testifying before the House Committee on Merchant Marine, Radio and Fisheries, Henry Adams Bellows, then vice president of the Columbia Broadcasting System, and before that one of the first of the Federal Radio Commissioners, observed:

"Mr. Aylesworth told you this morning—and said it rather ruefully—that the National Broadcasting Company did not have contracts with all of its associated stations. We do. . . .

"The basis of those contracts is this: we give the

non-commercial service of the Columbia to the station free of charge. That means substantially ten to twelve hours a day of broadcasts of the best programs that are anywhere available. . . . In return, the station gives us a preferential option on its time for commercial programs over the Columbia Broadcasting System and agrees that on two weeks written notice—there are minor variations in the contracts . . . it will so adjust its local schedule as to provide for our commercial programs."

The National Broadcasting Company's contracts are now similar to Columbia's, but in the early days, members of the NBC chains were charged for "sustaining" programs, and were not required to reserve any special hours for the network or commercial programs. Frequently, when NBC had sold time to national advertisers, there were nasty rows with its members who had sold the same hours to local advertisers.

When William Samuel Paley appeared on the scene in 1928 affairs at Columbia were in fairly good order, but the National Broadcasting Company had no cause to worry about competition. NBC had prestige, a treasury which the General Electric and the Westinghouse companies kept full, an advantageous contract with the Bell Sys-

tem and the stations with the best wave lengths.
Columbia was poor and it had to take the stations
that NBC did not want. Mr. Paley's triumph is
a success story of the millionaire who made good.

He was born heir to the business of the Congress Cigar Co., manufacturers of La Palina
cigars, famous in the radio world for the success
of the "La Palina Smokers," one of the outstanding commercial programs of the late 1920's. The
way sales jumped as a result of the radio advertising settled William Paley's future. At twenty-
seven he was rich, and radio broadcasting sounded
to him like a golden investment. Louchheim was
ready to sell part of his holdings, and Paley, his
father, and his brother-in-law, Dr. Levy, were
ready to buy. Paley's original investment by
which he became the dominant stockholder is
estimated at $300,000, and his total to date at
over a million and a half.

Except for the representatives of the bankers
and Louchheim, the board of directors of CBS
is a family affair. Besides William S., there are
Samuel and Jacob Paley, Isaac D. Levy and
Dr. Leon Levy. Dr. Levy supplies an interesting
link between Columbia and its chief rival, the

National Broadcasting Company. Dr. Levy is director of station WCAU, Columbia's Philadelphia outlet; in 1936, he was also the director of KYW, a Westinghouse station which is the Philadelphia unit of the National Broadcasting Company's Red Network. This was certainly carrying to an extreme Philadelphia's reputation for brotherly love. Apparently Dr. Levy was not troubled by the Gilbertian situation which forced him to compete with himself for business and to further the interests of NBC, when he is a major stockholder and a member of the board of its chief rival. There is another indirect tie-up between the two networks. Herbert B. Swope, brother of Gerald Swope, head of the General Electric Company, serves as director and as a member of the CBS executive committee. Until the spring of 1936 he was also chairman of the board of Keith-Albee-Orpheum, a subsidiary of the Radio-Keith-Orpheum Corporation of which Mr. Aylesworth was chairman.

The bankers' representatives were added to the CBS board after the financiers had put up the cash required to buy back control of the network from Paramount. The firms which helped with

this and subsequent financing, and which for their
efforts were given approximately 50 percent of
CBS Class A stock, are Brown Bros., Harriman
& Company, W. E. Hutton & Co. and Lehman
Brothers. Under an agreement dated March 7,
1932, between Columbia and Brown Bros., the
banking firm, acting in behalf of itself and others,
bought 18,246 shares of Class A stock for
$1,500,003 and were given an option on an addi-
tional block consisting of 6,082 shares. This
option was later exercised.[8] The banker's representatives on the board are Prescott S. Bush,
partner in Brown Bros., Joseph A. W. Iglehart,
partner in Hutton & Co., and Dorsey Richardson
of the Lehman firm. Except that Brown Bros.
were on Morgan's preferred list, there appears to
be no tie-up with the House of Morgan.

The history of Columbia illustrates the danger
of treating a great radio chain merely as a profit-
making venture. It has been bartered back and
forth, first to the Columbia Phonograph Company, then to Louchheim, then to Paramount and
finally to the bankers. A minor item like the social
significance of control of the air can, of course,

8 House Report 1273, 1935.

play no part in finance. So far, the bankers and the other members of the board have been well satisfied with President Paley and his policies.

"Mr. Paley, as a business man," writes *Fortune*, "is a theme that practically brings tears to the eyes of his directors—never in all their lives, they say, have they been associated with anybody so clever at business. Not only is he a master advertiser and feeler of the public pulse, but these gentlemen say that he is the greatest organizer, the best executive, the quickest thinker, the coolest negotiator they have ever seen."

President Paley has always understood the value of political connections. To head the department of station relations, he selected Sam Pickard described by *Fortune* as "the brightest commissioner." Pickard resigned as a Federal Radio Commissioner to take the Columbia job. In 1933, he added to his executive personnel Henry Adams Bellows, former radio commissioner, and a classmate at Harvard of Franklin D. Roosevelt. Vice President Bellows was placed in charge of Columbia's Washington station WJSV, and proved a most useful ambassador of CBS in Washington during the first days of the New Deal. Both Bellows and Pickard have now resigned. But even though the two former radio commissioners are no longer on active duty, the network stands in well with the Federal Communications Commission and has received many favors from it.

In the trade, and among the radio audience, Columbia has a reputation for being more liberal than its rival, the NBC. A good deal of this liberalism is, of course, good showmanship. Paley keeps in close touch with what the people want, and what Washington wants, and he knows how to make and to carry out a popular gesture.

THE MUTUAL BROADCASTING COMPANY

The Mutual Broadcasting System has not yet given the major networks any real competition. It holds three clear channels, one through Station WLW of Cincinnati which is a member of both NBC and the Mutual systems. Its $1,600,000 gross income for 1935-36, its second year of operation, is a good enough record, but it does not compare with the joint gross of $48,000,000 reported by the two major chains. Both the National Broadcasting Company and the Columbia Broadcasting System are worried, however, by the expansion of Mutual into a coast-to-coast network.

Mutual is the first coöperatively owned broadcasting system. According to its president, Wilbert E. Macfarlane (business manager of the *Chicago Tribune*), "the stations run Mutual instead of being run by the chains." Its basic network is composed of the Bamberger Department Store station WOR of Newark, New Jersey; the *Chicago Tribune's* radio outlet WGN; and the 500,000-watt station WLW of Cincinnati, most powerful in the country, owned by Powel Crosley, Jr., manufacturer of radio sets, ice boxes, etc.

So far as the public is concerned, Mutual leaves much to be desired. Among the sponsors, whose endorsements it proudly advertises, is the fascist organization, The Crusaders. WOR has offered a haven to several advertisers of patent medicine including Feen-a-mint and California Syrup of Figs which left Columbia after it banned laxative advertising.

When Mutual grows older, and stronger, it will undoubtedly be unwilling to play the rôle of poor relation, and to take programs which the two major networks have refused. In 1936, however, it enabled the public to hear many programs which otherwise would not have been on any network.

IV

MONEY TALKS

THE power and influence of our industrial and financial rulers in the broadcasting world is most clearly evidenced by the leeway permitted their spokesmen. Representatives of the major political parties, world-famous economists, and philosophers may be prevented, "in the public interest," from discussing particular subjects, or from talking at all. But Fred G. Clark of The Crusaders or J. A. Arnold of the American Taxpayers League are not similarly hamstrung.

For these men and their brethren carry the message of the industrialists to the people. Of course the radio audience does not know who is supporting the voice that has come to be their political, economic, and social adviser. Some of them send in their dimes, quarters and dollars in response to the plea for funds to carry on the weekly sermons, and since they are helping to pay, they grow more responsive. Few stop to

57

think that the dimes could not support the radio campaign, and even after public testimony is given showing that the Du Ponts, the Sloans and a group of their millionaire friends are paying the bills, there are still enough people in the radio audience who have been sufficiently mesmerized by the voice to make it worthwhile to continue.

The radio audience is not entirely to blame. When Fred Clark was on the air, you could positively hear the American flag waving in the breeze. It made you click your heels and raise your hand in salute. No, nothing has been said of the fascist salute. Not yet, in any event. Commander Clark spoke about the reds, the yellows, and the true blues. He talked about teachers' oaths, the wisdom of the Supreme Court, the folly of the Triple A policy, and against the TVA and the holding-company bills. Not a few of these subjects are controversial, but all of them are interesting to the members of the radio audience who want to "keep up with things," who have found it socially important during the last few years to be able to mouth a few words on economics and politics. It was such a useful

thing to listen to Commander Clark, and so convenient to be able to repeat his opinions.

It is this blind faith, this atrophy of the critical faculties which make our radio lobbyists a
menace. In the United States we have never been
free of the spokesmen for special interests. But
formerly they concentrated their efforts on our
legislators; they made no attempt to sail under
false colors. As far as such things could be, the
business was carried on in the open.

Today we have a new kind of lobbyist—the
Clark type. Neither officially, nor even unofficially, is he the accredited representative of the
men whose interests he serves. He harangues the
public, presumably of his own free will, and because of his impelling patriotism. Few in his
audience, and those few listen only for the cynical
pleasure derived, know whom he represents. The
great majority cannot, or will not, add two and
two together. They are told to write to their
congressmen, urging favorable action on certain
bills, unfavorable action on others. The radio
audience writes by the thousands.

The business men and bankers who so gener-
ously support The Crusaders and other lobbyists

are sufficiently shrewd to place the proper valuation on the use of radio as a propaganda instrument. Apparently they are completely contemptuous of the intelligence of their audience, for even though the disclosures of the Senate Committee's investigation of lobbying activities were given considerable publicity in the press in 1935–36, they continue to support these publicly discredited organizations. Eight years before Senator Black's committee began to hold its hearings, Senator Caraway was chairman of a similar investigation of lobbying organizations. Of J. A. Arnold, whose American Taxpayers' League was also investigated by Senator Black, it was observed: "How business men of ordinary sagacity can be induced to contribute to Arnold's purposes is entirely inexplicable to your committee. . . ." The answer is that business has found that through Arnold, Clark and other flag-waving patriots, desired purposes can be accomplished.

Especially since radio can be made the spearhead of propaganda campaigns, it is more worthwhile than ever to support these patriots in style. The rulers in the fascist states give credit to radio as the greatest propaganda tool yet perfected. Americans who seek to control the government and the people—who are building a true-blue type of fascism in the United States—know that the instrument most worthwhile owning and playing on is the radio.

So while our educators continue to argue among themselves how best to use the radio to instruct and enlighten the people, the propagandist for our industrial and financial rulers has perfected the technique of using the radio to confuse and prejudice the people. And while our broadcasting companies have ordinarily adopted a holier than thou attitude in the censorship of controversial subjects, they have both given free time and sold time to the propagandist who speaks for our still half-baked fascists.

As a specimen of this new type of lobbying, let us examine Mr. Clark's organization, The Crusaders. Organized in 1929 to advocate the repeal of the Eighteenth Amendment, its activities were increased in 1933 by the additions to its charter of section 5, "To oppose all forces destructive to sound government," and section 6, "To do all lawful things necessary, incidental or appropriate, to the carrying out of the purposes aforesaid." Except for the broad interpretation that can be placed on the words "all forces destructive to sound government" these additions do not appear to be fraught with danger or significance. Even today, the average law-abiding citizen who believes in the democratic form of government, in the rule of the people, might conceivably be in agreement with the principle laid down in The Crusaders' amended constitution. That is, if he did not know how these provisions had been interpreted and carried out.

Commander Clark, who testified before the Black Committee that "I am not an expert at anything," was sufficiently astute to recognize the importance of the radio in carrying on his propaganda against the destructive forces. Radio, indeed, has always been the spearhead of his efforts. Even though arrangements had been made for free time on the Columbia network he immediately began to raise a fund for his radio work. James F. Bell, chairman of General Mills, Inc., a company that spends a fortune every year for radio advertising, was one of the first of the busy business men who was willing to play the good angel. Not only did he promise to help in the fund raising, but to show his kindly feelings, he himself donated $5,876 to the cause. The amount itself did not stagger Commander Clark. A week before he had received the identical sum from E. T. Weir, chairman of the Weirton Steel Company. He had also received $2,500 from Lester Armour, vice president of Armour & Co., $5,000 from Clifford S. Heinz of the fifty-seven varieties, another $5,000 from Paul Moore of the American Can Co. and National Biscuit Co., and still another $5,000 from F. B. Wells, vice president of F. H. Peavey & Co., grain-elevator operators. A few days later Irenée Du Pont's contribution of $5,000 came in. With this money, and with this list of sponsors, Commander Clark, who still had not named himself the Voice of The Crusaders, had a good start toward representing the people.

To handle the funds that were pouring in to carry on the radio campaign, three trustees were appointed, Ralph A. Bard, investment banker, R. Douglas Stuart, vice president of Quaker Oats, and Edward Ryerson of the Ryerson Steel

Company. Under the trust agreement it was provided that:

"Said funds shall be used and expended at present for the purpose of arranging for a series of radio talks by a speaker to be approved by the trustee."

During his testimony before the Black Committee, Commander Clark stated that he had never seen the trust agreement. This, to say the least, was careless, because if he intended to represent the people, he certainly should have known the power that his contributors had to control what he could say. But even if he were familiar with the terms of the trust agreement, it still would have made little difference to Fred Clark. Nobody, according to his testimony given under oath, had the right to dictate what the Voice would say.

The senate investigators were not convinced and by direct cross examination attempted to get nearer the truth.

The Chairman: Is it your judgment that if you had made a speech for the TVA, for the Wheeler-Rayburn bill, and for the banking bill, and to put a tax on high incomes and high inheritances that these trustees would have permitted you to continue to speak?

Mr. Clark: They might have tried to stop it.

The Chairman: But they did have a right to stop it if you did not say what they wanted said? They had a right to do it, didn't they?

Mr. Clark: They had a right to try to.

The Chairman: They had a right to cut out the payments?

Mr. Clark: All right; they had a right to cut out the payments. They could not have stopped us.

The Chairman: Did you have any other funds to buy the radio time?

Mr. Clark: We have not any funds now, but we are going on.

The Chairman: Are you still paying that much for the radio?

Mr. Clark: Yes, sir.

The Chairman: Who is paying for it now?

Mr. Clark: The contributions we get through our appeals over the radio.

The Chairman: Have you a list of them?

The contributors who had heard the radio appeals for funds to carry on the crusading work during the weeks of February 1–15, 1935, included G. M. Moffett, president of the Corn Products Refining Company, who helped along with a check for $2,500; J. H. Pew of the Sun Oil Company, who contributed another $2,500;

Henry M. Dawes, who sent in a mere $100; Ernest Mahle, one of the unknown radio audience who chipped in $25; E. M. Allen, president of the Mathieson Alkali works and the International Cement Corporation, who sent along a check for $100; George A. Ball, president of the Ball Glass Works Co., who raised the ante with his contribution of $2,000; W. C. Teagle, president of the Standard Oil Co. of New Jersey, who lowered it again with a contribution of $200 which was followed by a $500 donation by Eugene G. Grace, president of the Bethlehem Steel Co. Then there was a check from another member of the radio audience, William A. Read, for $50, and the same amount from Edwin L. Webster of the Stone & Webster bond house. One of the last contributors during this period was Irene Jackson Sloan, wife of the president of General Motors, who donated $1,250.

Even after this list had been read into the record, Commander Clark insisted that he represented the little fellow, that he was talking for the "peepul" and that no one could exert any influence over the Voice. This professed innocence of the facts of life is appalling in a man who undertakes to direct and mold public opinion.

Exactly how the contributors influenced the Voice is shown clearly enough on the record. On May 27, The Crusaders' Commander received the following communication from Fred W. Blaisdell, his co-worker, and the man in charge of the Chicago headquarters.

"Our friends in Detroit are after me hot and heavy for The Crusaders to get busy on the Wagner bill. Of course, we will run into opposition from a part of organized labor if we do this, but I believe a sound argument can be developed that the Wagner bill is the most dangerous measure to labor itself of any bill now pending in Congress."

Two days later, Commander Clark sent a telegram to Blaisdell:

"We made a hurried effort to get out a broadcast for tomorrow night on the subject of taxes, in order to show what the trends mean to the individual, which we intended to revise this morning on our return. In the meantime, Bell was here yesterday and he and Peed left word that they wanted us to attack the TVA tomorrow night. . . ."

The man who grew indignant when the senators suggested that he might be influenced by his contributors apparently adopted a more realistic attitude at other times. Mr. Bell was in every respect a valuable man to the organization; he wanted an immediate attack on the TVA and the Commander dutifully complied. The harangue against the Wagner bill had to wait for another time. On the following evening, the Voice spoke on "Expensive Governmental Duplication":

"In every district where the Federal Government is building power plants there already exist private operating companies with equipment capable of generating from 30 to 50 percent more electricity than the consumers in the district have ever used or are using now. Think that over."

The Voice always urged the audience to think over the "information" which it supplied. This is in line with Mr. Clark's definition of the express purpose of his organization—"to clarify public thinking."

Senator Schwellenbach suggested that the audience might have had more interesting food for thought if during this broadcast, or during the more famous one, "Choose your Colors," when the Voice declared: "We neither ask for nor receive any advice from any public-utility officials or public-utility corporations. . . . We did not receive a dollar in contributions from any public-utility company. We should immediately return it had we received one," they had been informed that Sewell Avery, a director of the Commonwealth Edison Co. and the Peoples Gas, Light & Coke Co., had donated $5,000; that Thomas E. Donnelly, another director of the Commonwealth Edison Company, had given $1,000; that A. W. Robertson, chairman of the board of the Westinghouse Electric & Manufacturing Co., had contributed $1,000; that F. A. Merrick, president of the same company, had given $876; that Sutherland Dows of the Iowa Electric Light & Power Co. had given still another $1,000; and that Albert P. Lasker, president of Lord & Thomas, an advertising agency for the public utility interests, had given $5,000.

Mr. Clark hedged and pleaded ignorance. When the checks came in, he did not ask the business connections of the gentlemen who had been good enough to contribute. He was smart enough, however, to talk many times about the dangers to the little stockholder and to the consumer of electric current of permitting the government to go into competition with the private utilities.

Besides taking orders from the public utilities and the banking interests, Commander Clark was also apparently under the thumb of the omnipresent Mr. Hearst. Sherman Rogers, a member of The Crusaders' New York staff, and the man who wrote many of the speeches which the Voice broadcast, was a former Hearstling, but the Lord of San Simeon exerted a more direct influence. Mr. Hearst could be very helpful in supplying newspaper publicity, and The Crusaders for this reason alone were in no position to offend him. On such an important matter as the bonus it was therefore necessary for them to change their point of view, in order to retain the good will of the Hearst press. Originally, the Voice had intended to speak against the bonus, but after a wire from Blaisdell at the Chicago headquarters that "Our disapproval of bonus bill will lose us support of one nationwide newspaper chain," Commander Clark decided that it was best to eliminate the discussion. At the investigation, Blaisdell identified the chain as ". . . quite probably—the Hearst newspapers."

At least as amazing as the donation of five months' free time by the Columbia Broadcasting System is the fact that The Crusaders have been able to continue with their program after the publicity given to the findings of the Black Committee. During the senatorial hearing, Commander Clark promised that he would report to his radio audience on the findings and evidence, particularly in regard to the contributors through whose generosity he had been able to broadcast. Some of the senators gave expression to their incredulity, but Commander Clark was as good as his word. On April 20, only a week after the investigation, Clark had his speech ready. After implying that the Black Committee was attempting to discredit only organizations unfriendly to the Roosevelt administration, Commander Clark undertook to explain away the disclosures which possibly might have troubled some members of his audience.

"Answering question number one regarding possible contributors' influence on Crusaders' broadcasts, permit me to explain that in October, 1934, a group of men met in Chicago at my request to consider the advisability of delivering a series of broadcasts on constitutional questions and economic facts. A substantial sum was pledged at that meeting. Not one word was spoken about public utilities or public utility legislation, banks or bank legislation. . . .

"Answering question number two, as to why we had not broadcast to the country the names of our contributors. In the first place, it would have taken at least six broadcasts of fifteen minutes each to give the names of the contributors alone. The man who gave from fifty cents to one dollar would have been just as much entitled to have his name mentioned as the contributor who gave one thousand dollars or more. . . ."

In all fairness it may have been only right to honor the little fellow by reading his name out loud along with that of the Du Ponts and Sloans. But after all, were there so many little fellows, Mr. Clark, and don't you think that they would have been so keenly interested in hearing the names of the real financiers that they would have been satisfied not to have their own listed?

Even if any skeptical members of the radio audience had taken the trouble to write a letter and raise these points, Commander Clark would not have been troubled. He still had his contract with the Mutual Broadcasting System, and the broadcasting officials had made no move to exercise their option and terminate the contract. In itself, the history of The Crusaders' dealings with the broadcasting companies is significant. The first series of radio speeches were broadcast by the Columbia Broadcasting System free of charge. According to Clark's testimony, the normally astute Mr. Paley was a sucker in this instance. He was never informed who was back of the organization, who were the contributors, nor how much money was being collected as a result of the radio broadcasts. Mr. Paley's generosity and lack of curiosity continued for five months ending on April 30, 1935. Even before the five months were up, however, Mr. Paley was apparently growing restive, for on April 1, Commander Clark sent off the following telegram:

"On good advice here request not addressing letter to Paley but to Columbia Broadcasting System, 485 Madison Avenue, New York. However, get important people to send letters to Paley, flattering him on the constructive work he is doing in offering The Crusader broadcasts."

This scheme did not work. Either Mr. Paley would not be flattered, or he had become curious and a little uneasy about the propaganda he was a party in disseminating. The Crusaders were thus placed in the unfortunate position of having to use some of their funds to pay for time on the air.

Considering the rigidity with which minor chains as well as the major chains censor program material, it might seem that The Crusaders would have found it difficult to arrange for broadcasting facilities. But this was not the case. The Mutual Broadcasting System was quite ready to take The Crusaders' money, and to broadcast their message. Although this system did not give The Crusaders the vast audience which they had enjoyed during the free time on the Columbia network, it was nevertheless a good enough start. To the Mutual stations, The Crusaders added Mr. Shephard's Yankee network (then affiliated with Columbia), and WIND of Chicago. Mr. Shephard is the gentleman who refused to broadcast Earl Browder's speech when the Columbia Broadcasting System arranged the first national hook-up for a Communist.

At the time that the Black Committee was investigating the activities of The Crusaders, they had built up a nice network to carry the crusading message to the people. Besides the Bamberger Department Store station WOR, and Crosley's (no labor-strike news) WLW of the Mutual System, they were broadcasting over the Yankee network's two stations, WAAB and WPRO, over the Don Lee station KFRC of San Francisco, WIP of Philadelphia, KTAR of Phoenix, Arizona, and the American Federation of Labor station, WCFL of Chicago. None of these stations immediately terminated the contracts which had been made to carry the Voice of Big Business. The Commander continued to give the clarion cry—"Wake up, America!"—until September, 1936. Then it was taken up by Andrew F. Kelly who continued The Crusaders' program as The Horse-sense Philosopher over WOR, the two Hearst stations, WBAL of Baltimore and WCAE of Pittsburgh, WRVA of Richmond and WGAR of Cleveland, all members of the National Broadcasting Company's networks, WGR of Buffalo affiliated with the Columbia network, and KLW of Detroit, of the Mutual System.

The life and work of The Crusaders have been considered in detail because this organization is an outstanding example of the industrialists'-bankers' radio propaganda instruments. But there are many others which under a thin disguise of patriotism plead the cause of the vested interests. The appeal is always to passion and prejudice. Like the Voice of The Crusaders which alternated praise for the private public utilities with horrendous tales of the red menace, the other voices of Big Business raise the red scare, the black scare, any color scare in fact which keeps the passions of the audience running high.

Unlike The Crusaders, such organizations as the Southern Committee to Uphold the Constitution, the American Taxpayers League, the Sentinels of the Republic, and the others which are fed by the same hands, do not depend solely on the radio to carry on their subversive propaganda, but take to the air only on special occasions. Many of them are still so old-fashioned that they prefer to use the press to the air waves. Their own little success in broadcasting, and the bigger success of The Crusaders will, however, undoubtedly influence them in their future activities.

John H. Kirby, that "lovely old gentleman" [1] who is president of the Southern Committee to Uphold the Constitution, the organization responsible for the circulation at Governor Gene Talmadge's Macon convention of the newspaper showing Mrs. Roosevelt being squired by two Negroes, was just a bit too old-fashioned to place much faith in the radio. Governor Talmadge, however, understands its propaganda value, and the Macon speech was broadcast. The funds for this grand celebration were largely contributed by John J. Raskob and P. S. Du Pont.

J. A. Arnold, guiding spirit of the American Taxpayers' League, one of the flag-waving organizations that compete for contributions from the Du Pont boys and their friends, was one of the first to use the radio to broadcast its propaganda. Despite the big names on his list of contributors, Mr. Arnold's organization must be rated among the small fry. The good days for

[1] So described by Vance Muse, one of his co-workers, to the Black Committee.

him were back in 1932, the year his organization was incorporated. The National Broadcasting Company broadcast the message of this professional lobbyist seventy-seven times, free of charge, the last broadcast being in 1933. Why they stopped, it is hard to say; certainly they could not only then have discovered what interests Arnold represented, and what his purposes were. During the Caraway investigation of lobbying in 1928, Arnold had been thoroughly exposed as a professional propagandist. Perhaps the network's representatives did not keep up with what was happening. Or perhaps it was W. L. Mellon's interest in the American Taxpayers' League which made the broadcasts over the National Broadcasting System possible. By 1932, Westinghouse's ownership of the Radio Corporation of America and the National Broadcasting System had legally and officially been brought to an end. Mr. Mellon, however, is a director of the Westinghouse Company, one of whose stations is KDKA of Pittsburgh. This station, and others in the Westinghouse chain, are members of the NBC network. Mr. Arnold was thus able to arrange through the good graces of Mr. Mellon for the facilities of KDKA, and for other stations. Altogether, through what Mr. Arnold termed "local contacts," he was able to build a chain of forty-three stations which broadcast his messages. Even though Andrew W. contributed only $1,000 to the cause, the Mellons proved to be good and valuable friends.

Bainbridge Colby also provided valuable assistance by arranging for free time on Hearst's New York station, WINS, and also for publicity in the Hearst press. But E. Parmlee Prentice, son-in-law of Mr. Rockefeller, Sr., was the largest contributor, with a donation of $1,500.

Unlike Commander Clark of The Crusaders, Mr. Arnold did not elect himself star radio performer. However, he sought instead the services of such public speakers as Colonel McCormick of the *Chicago Tribune* and Governor Gene Talmadge of Georgia. But all of them, no matter what the subject, harped more or less on one string. Taxes had to be reduced; that is, the taxes which were a burden to Big Business and the money rulers. The American Taxpayers' League were in favor of state sales taxes as a substitute for corporation taxes, high income taxes, gift taxes or, as Senator Minton summed it up, "you were in favor of taking all these taxes off the big fellows and putting a sales tax on a loaf of bread."

Certainly, this was a program which the Mellons, the Raskobs and their friends should gladly have supported. They did, to a certain point. If Mr. Arnold had continued his radio program, he might have fared better financially. But since 1933 he has attempted no lobbying on the air, and his influence with our legislators is not great. So the business men have sent their contributions to The Crusaders, whose national commander may have no influence with the legislators, but whose voice can influence the people.

Besides the misinformation which Clark popularized during the years he was on the air, he has by his surprising "popular" success set an example that the lobbyist, interested in lining his own pockets, as well as in being of service to the money rulers, will attempt to emulate. Mr. Clark himself received in cash only $5,754.16 for the period from May, 1935, to April, 1936, or $523 a month "to cover his expenses." Mr. Dickie, director of the Eastern Division office,

however, received a salary of $207 a week, while
Fred W. Blaisdell, the business manager, got
along on $400 a month. The financial possibilities
in the operation of such a "nonpartisan, nonfac-
tional, nonracial organization" as The Crusaders
are seen to be interesting.

But even assuming that the lobbyist and his
assistants are in no way concerned with financial
gain, they will still turn to the radio to spread
their propaganda. The power of the radio has
been tried and proved and the broadcasting companies have established a precedent of open-
mindedness. And if the stations' representatives
should grow timid, or recalcitrant, there are
enough methods by which the propagandist and
the men for whom he talks can apply the screws.
Many of the financial backers of our professional
flag wavers are among the biggest radio advertisers on the air. Neither the Du Ponts, nor the
Sloans of General Motors, nor even Mr. Bell of
General Mills can be offended. Besides, men who
are more directly connected with the radio world
must be reckoned with. We have seen how Mr.
Mellon was able to help along the broadcasting
campaign of the American Taxpayers' League.

So far, the Sentinels of the Republic, another of the lobbying organizations, have carried on their campaign through the movies and the press, but if they should decide to turn to the radio, they may find a good friend in General Harbord, chairman of the Board of the Radio Corporation of America, who is also on the executive committee of the Sentinels.

The possibilities that radio opens to the propagandist are utterly terrifying. Tonight, The Crusaders will again be on the air; next week, the voice may be multiplied by two. And week after week, month after month, the spokesmen for the money rulers, hiding behind the name of patriotism, or of some other ism, will pour their misinformation, their perverted facts, their downright lies into the ears of the radio audience.

Considering the use that the power trust and the other money rulers have made of the press, considering the success that they have already had with the broadcasting companies, it is not to be expected that their propagandists will be banned from the air waves. Then how is this subversive material to be controlled? The answer, and an entirely unsatisfactory one, is only by the final censorship of the radio audience itself. Only by turning the dial, only by refusing to listen to these fake patriots, can their rising power be checked. Only if Americans heed the single piece of good advice that Mr. Clark has broadcast and "wake up," can this real threat to democracy be wiped out.

V

THE MEDICINE MEN'S SHOW

H ELLO, everybody! Would you like to have one of the thrills of your life?" The radio salesman pauses significantly. "Try Kolynos toothpaste."

"Beautiful ladies! Do you wish that your hands were white as alabaster, then use Blah Blah lotion, a little every morning, a little every evening. Rub some on before you wash the dishes and after you wash the dishes, before you give baby his bath, before you meet the girls for a game of bridge. And now I introduce Miss High Note, the youngest star of the Metropolitan Opera Company. R-e-m-e-m-b-e-r [slow crescendo] Blah Blah lotion for beautiful hands. Send in five labels and we'll forward a generous free sample of Blah Blah hand lotion. Send in fifty labels and you will receive a little book telling all about Blah Blah products. And here's a secret. Do you know that Miss High Note never uses any creams but Blah Blah's? And now, let's get on with the show."

Criticism of the commercial announcements, of the incongruity of combining operatic music with hand lotions and mouthwashes (for an entire season performances of the Metropolitan Opera Company were broadcast through the courtesy of Listerine) is waved aside as rank ingratitude. Remember, friends of the radio audience, that business men pay the bill for broadcasting, and that the commercial sponsors are the keystone of our "free" radio. Who would support the industry were the business men to withdraw their patronage? Would you have it dependent on the government? Would you be willing to help meet the cost of broadcast entertainment by paying a tax? Well then, be grateful for favors received.

The commercial announcements may be boring, or distasteful, they may embody all the chicanery of the old medicine man's show, but after all, business is not spending a fortune every year merely to "entertain" you.

A half-hour broadcast by the twenty-one stations that comprise the basic Red Network of the National Broadcasting Company costs $4,800;

the cost of the twenty-one basic stations of the Blue Network is $4,320; for the twenty-four stations on Columbia's basic hookup the bill is $5,085. These are the minimum prices for network advertising and include the charges only for those stations which it is mandatory for the network advertiser to use. Many advertisers buy the facilities of the entire Red Network, for which the price per half hour is $11,270, or of the Blue at $10,484, while customers of the Columbia Broadcasting System who wish national coverage use all the stations in the System, for which the charge is $11,960. For an hour's broadcast the price is slightly less than twice the charge for a half hour, and for a quarter hour, a little more than half the price for a thirty-minute broadcast. These are the prices for broadcasting after six P.M. when the greatest number of listeners are "tuned in." After eleven P.M. rates are reduced by approximately half, and the half-rate scale is also used for daytime hours. For network advertising the rates are figured on the basis of current local time in each city. Of course, no advertiser can expect a single broadcast to increase sales. The hour, half-hour and quarter-hour periods must be bought regularly, at least once a week, more frequently twice or three times weekly.

For the first six months of 1936, the Columbia Broadcasting System reported that the average expenditure by advertisers for radio time was $145,270—a gain of some forty-odd thousand dollars over the year before. On the National Broadcasting Company's networks, the big spenders were also increasing their budgets, and the number of companies that paid in excess of $350,000 to the networks' stations more than doubled. These figures do not include the cost of "talent" which may be as much or more than the charges of the radio station.

Many of our most popular radio stars received their early training in Hollywood and for their services on the air they ask Hollywood prices. According to government statistics for the year 1935, commercial sponsors spent $50,000,000 or just short of $1,000,000 a week for "talent." This bill, it was estimated, would be increased by at least 10 percent for 1936–37. Some sponsors are beginning to object to the high cost of radio advertising, but still they must "keep up with the Joneses." If their competitors' wares are being

ballyhooed by a high-priced "artist," they also
must have a star who is equally popular. Thus
the price is maintained; the supply of radio talent,
believe it or not, is unequal to the demand.

It pays to be a popular radio star. Consider
the following reported earnings:

PERFORMER	WEEKLY SALARY	SPONSOR
Major Bowes	$25,000	Chrysler Motor Corporation
Eddie Cantor	10,000	Texaco
Burns & Allen	10,000	Grapenuts (General Foods)
Fred Waring	10,000	Ford Motor Company
Jack Benny	7,500	Jell-O
Guy Lombardo	5,000	Bond Bread
Lucretia Bori	10,000	(2 performances) Ford Motor Company
Ed Wynn	3,000	Spud Cigarettes
Phil Baker	2,500	Gulf Oil Corporation
Jessica Dragonette	2,000	Colgate-Palmolive-Peet Company

These salaries are not all sheer profit. Some of
the contracts provide that the stars pay for all
incidental "talent" included on the program—
Major Bowes, for example, always had to pay

his "amateurs." But even after these bills have been subtracted, the headliner's weekly check for services rendered is still written in four figures.

Although some sponsors, like Henry Ford, camouflage their radio advertising as a public service, the great majority make no pretense that it is anything but a direct sales effort. Not only are the "free" shows introduced by and concluded with long-winded commercial announcements, but the advertised product is mentioned half a dozen times, or more, during the show itself. For a long time Jack Benny spoke so much about his sponsor's product that he seemed to be sinking in a sea of Jell-O, while the programs of Burns and Allen, before their services were bought by the General Foods Company, were 50 percent Campbell's Tomato Juice. No longer is it possible to escape the advertising announcements by tuning in late on the program, and tuning out early; the advertising announcements are part of the show. Thus has broadcasting effected a union between business and the "arts." Clowns, whose business was once only to be funny, are now super, super salesmen whose skill is measured by the merchandise it sells.

The sponsors still pretend that the radio entertainment is supplied at no cost to the listener. It is the same old game. Strangely enough, the average member of the radio audience does not realize that he is paying the cost of his entertainment in the price of the product. If he thinks of the cost of advertising at all, he usually observes that business is probably spending its advertising appropriation on radio rather than in newspapers and magazines, and if this means that he gets free entertainment, he's all for it. In some instances, John Public is right, but the bill for radio advertising is steadily increasing, and this increase cannot be met by cutting the cost of other advertising. How is this difference made up? Obviously, since Big Business is not engaged in public philanthropy, the public must pay.

But the flimflamming of the public about "free entertainment" is actually of less importance than the control over the public mind and tastes that radio advertising has given business. An industrialist who wishes to explain his "philosophy" buys a national hookup. The same facilities are available to the vendors of patent medicines. Men who formerly might never have gotten a hearing now address the hundred million guinea pigs in their own homes.

Since the primary purpose of broadcast entertainment is to sell merchandise, the programs must appeal to the many—not to the few. They are planned, as one radio executive explained, for an audience whose intelligence "cannot be underestimated."

Sales are increased by the crooners, the human-relations "courts" and the hick playlets, and therefore such entertainment will be continued. Some members of the radio audience may be difficult to please and, for example, turn the switch when the Alka-Seltzer program goes on the air. They dislike the vaudeville act, and the patent medicine it advertises. But there are others who are more receptive. One of the trade journals recounts a little story to indicate just how grateful the audience may be. A nice old couple perched themselves on stools at a drugstore soda fountain and ordered glasses of Alka-Seltzer. Neither tasted the widely advertised beverage, but after toying with the glasses for a few minutes, the old gentleman called for his check. Someone in the radio business was standing by and after the proper apologies asked why the drinks had been bought but not consumed. The old gentleman explained that neither he nor his wife liked Alka-Seltzer nor felt the need of alkalizing, but they did like the sponsored radio program and to show their appreciation, they bought two glasses of Alka-Seltzer every week.

Unquestionably, the nice old couple represent an extreme of gratitude. There are, however, thousands who drink Alka-Seltzer every day, who rub Vicks on their chests, who eat Ex-Lax "when nature forgets," not to show gratitude for free entertainment but because they have been convinced by the radio salesman that they can cure the real or imaginary ills that beset them with patent medicines. Testifying before the Federal Communications Commission in the spring of 1935, Dr. Arthur J. Cramp of the American Medical Association declared:

"Many newspapers, as a matter of enlightened self-interest, have developed certain standards of decency and censorship that keep out of their pages the advertisements of many products of this character. Further, the public has through several generations developed a defense mechanism against the printed word and is much less likely to be carried away by false or fraudulent claims made in cold type than it is when similar claims are made verbally by a plausible radio announcer. Then, too, claims that are to be made in printed form have a permanency that causes the maker of them to be much more cautious than when they are to have the ephemeral character of a radio broadcast. It is also to be remembered that impressionable young people do not, as a rule, read 'patent medicine' advertisements in newspapers or magazines. These same people can hardly avoid listening to the 'patent medicine' ballyhoo that comes into their homes over the radio."

As examples of objectionable patent medicine advertising, Dr. Cramp cited that of Alka-Seltzer, the "antiacid" whose essential drug is aspirin. "A person who follows the directions and takes 16 tablets a day," said Dr. Cramp, "would consume over 70 grains of aspirin and over 6 grains of salicylic acid in that period." He also objected to the advertising of Peruna, a beverage containing 18 percent alcohol, as a digestive stimulator and a tonic for everyone; to that of Crazy Crystals, against which the United States Food and Drug Administration has proceeded eighteen times; to the claims made for Ex-Lax, "the delicious chocolate laxative that will not form a habit" although its purgative drug is phenolph-thalein; and to Willard Tablets, essentially baking powder, bismuth subnitrate and magnesium oxide, but advertised as a treatment for acid dyspepsia and stomach ulcers.

A year and a half after Dr. Cramp testified in Washington, all of the products that he specifically mentioned were still on the air. Some of them, like Ex-Lax, had gone from one of the major networks to the Mutual Broadcasting System, and others to individual stations, because the two major networks have become prudish about broadcasting the efficacy of laxatives and similar products.

Since May 13, 1935, the Columbia Broadcasting System has accepted no contracts for the advertising of products "which describe graphically or repellently any internal bodily functions, symptomatic results of internal disturbances, or matters which are generally not considered acceptable topics in social groups." Under this classification is listed laxatives, depilatories and deodorants. When this announcement was made, the National Broadcasting Company was piqued by all the praise garnered by its rival. In Decem-

ber of 1933, it pointed out, the NBC had instituted a policy of accepting no more laxative accounts (although those already on the network
had the option of remaining not only for the dura-
tion of their contracts but so long as the contracts
were renewed without interruption). A similar
restriction was placed on body deodorants in August of 1934. The catch, of course, was in the
privilege of renewal.

Despite the networks' rulings, the medicine
men and the merchants who sell beauty in pack-
ages still remain their best customers. For 1935,
advertising sponsored by drug and pharmaceuti-
cal manufacturers on the national networks increased by 27.9 percent. Of the nine advertisers
who spent more than a million dollars (exclusive
of "talent") for radio advertising in that year,
six are in the medico-cosmetic business. The biggest spender was Proctor & Gamble (Ivory,
Crisco, Chipso, etc.) with $2,105,237; next came
Colgate-Palmolive-Peet with $1,679,037; then
Sterling Products (Bayer's Aspirin, California
Syrup of Figs, Fletcher's Castoria, ZBT Baby
Powder, Dr. Lyon's Toothpowder) with $1,422,-
651, followed by American Home Products Com-

pany (Anacin, Bisodol, Kolynos) with $1,211,-
568; Lady Esther Company with $1,100,998,
and Pepsodent with $1,098,996. Of all of these
companies, Pepsodent (sponsor of Amos 'n'
Andy) was the only one whose 1935 budget was
not increased over the year before. There was,
in fact, a general increase in radio's medicine
shows. For regional networks this increase
amounted to 220.3 percent for drugs, and 328.4
percent for cosmetics. In 1936 every one of the
above companies increased its radio appropriation, and Dr. Miles' laboratories, makers of Alka-
Seltzer, were added to the list of advertisers
spending more than one million dollars on radio.

A cynic can find real amusement in the new
hold that the medicine men and the skin deep spe-
cialists have acquired over the public. While the
muckraking journalists have been exposing the
claims and exorbitant prices of the medicine-
cosmetic hawkers, the latter have been watching
their sales shoot up among the radio audience.

"The Quickest Way to a Woman's Lips Are Her
Ears!" advertised the Columbia Broadcasting System in
February, 1936, ten months after it had announced a
general reform of advertising on its network. "For women

listen to beauty advice. This is the unmysterious reason why Cosmetic manufacturers are so successful on the air. Women *listen* . . . and any Cosmetic manufacturer can get upward of 5,000,000 women *to listen at the same time* by using the facilities of the Columbia Network. Is there anything strange, then, that advertisers expect extraordinary results from CBS—and get them? Talk to 5,000,000 women at the same time about their beauty and your product—and something is bound to happen. What else but that the women will do some talking on their own account at the nearest drugstore? As drug manufacturers have already discovered, they listen (and talk) about their health, too. In fact, drug and cosmetic radio programs constitute the largest group of advertising on the air today. . . ."

Undoubtedly there is a growing skepticism about the efficacy of some of the much ballyhooed products, but there are still many people who are convinced by the glib-tongued radio salesmen that by swallowing enough pills, or using enough salves and lotions, they can cure anything from dandruff to stomach ulcers.

In one of the elaborate brochures published by the National Broadcasting Company for advertising agencies and the agencies' clients, the value of radio's emotional appeal is comprehensively described.

" 'What we try to do in our programs,' remarks a man whose chief radio experience has been with dramatic sketches, 'is to transport our listeners into some make-believe situation created by our story. If we are able to do this, we know we'll be able to get them excited and interested. For fifteen minutes, we have shut everything else out of their minds. At the end, when the announcer comes along with his talk, his audience has been "softened up" for him. No wonder he makes an impression.' " [1]

The radio advertisers have gone the limit to "soften up" the audience. There was, for example, the program of Ambrosia, broadcast over the NBC network. Ambrosia did nothing less than to provide the ladies of the radio audience with a lover. T. R. Carskadon, writing in the *New Republic,* has given the permanency of type to the gushing of the salesman-lover:

"Fair lady, have you a few minutes for someone who thinks you are the loveliest girl in the world? Lean over here close to your radio a minute—close to me—just as if I could look into your lovely eyes—scent the per-

[1] *Let's Look at Radio Together,* 1936.

fume of your hair—caress the velvety softness of your
cheek—darling—

"Darling—what are we going to call your radio here?
Our trysting place? Our rendezvous—you're so sweet
— Do you think you'll have a quarter hour for me tomorrow, say four o'clock. I'll be at your radio here—
my shrine—where I worship the loveliest girl in the
world."

The loveliest girls in the world were trans-
ported gently from the romantic to the real business of the afternoon, which was to sell bottles
of Ambrosia. Didn't they want to look their best
when they greeted their lover? Of course they
did. Then, advised their lover, buy Ambrosia at
any drug, department or ten-cent store.

The "Your Lover" broadcasts were back in
1934, but they have been followed by others
whose salesmen are equally sympathetic. In the
1935–36 season Kelvin Keech, who sold Sloan's
Liniment on the air, was described by the editor
of the Women's National Radio Committee bulletin as so sympathetic that "you have the feeling
he would gladly come over to massage a lame
arm."

In the same season General Mills, Inc. (Gold

Medal Flour) broadcast a religious program, entitled "Hymns of All Churches," for the more serious-minded ladies of the unseen audience. Five thousand clergymen of all faiths were asked to vote for their favorite hymns which would be combined with a "dignified and proper" sales announcement. The ladies liked the program, and the clergy found nothing incongruous in the combination of hymns and flour until Rev. Dr. Raymond Forman, preaching in St. Paul's Methodist Episcopal Church, New York, denounced the entire proceedings. Waxing exceeding wroth, he described a possible conference in the offices of General Mills:

"Smith says, 'Jones, how do you feel about the sales appeal in "Jesus, Lover of my Soul," or "Nearer my God to Thee"; or do you think "Holy Spirit, Heavenly Dove" or "Must Jesus Bear the Cross Alone?" would be more profitable?' "

Dr. Forman urged the members of his congregation to write to the sponsor and denounce the commercialization of the sacred hymns. After the sermon, the Secretary of the Greater New York Federation of Churches found that the series had started "with good intentions but had now turned into a commercial idea." At the time that Dr. Forman was urging his congregation to register its disapproval, five of the program's fifteen minutes was being used to extoll the virtues of Gold Medal Flour, and listeners who had been "softened up" by the hymns were urged to write for the booklet: *Food Men Hurry Home For.*

The protests of the clergy and of some members of the radio audience have not prevented other sponsors from using church music to advertise the merits of their products. In the summer of 1936 Ivory's claim to near purity (Ivory is 99 44/100 percent pure) was being sung to the accompaniment of hymns and amens and in the Easter season of 1937 the Adam Hat Company sponsored a broadcast of the Passion Play.

It is continually rumored that broadcast advertising is improving, and that radio no longer merits the description, "the cesspool of advertising." In its report for the fiscal year 1935, the Federal Communications Commission did not, however, substantiate the rumor. The Commissioners wrote:

"In the past fiscal year there has been a notable increase in complaints to the Commission of stations broadcasting objectionable programs. . . . Formal action was taken with regard to 226 separate objectionable programs broadcast over 152 stations. Some action was taken with regard to a much larger additional number of complaints. . . . The broadcasting of false, fraudulent, and misleading advertising in various guises has been the chief source of complaint. In many instances the Federal Trade Commission, the Post Office Department and the Food and Drug Administration had taken action to curtail the objectionable activities of medical advertisers in printed form, the result being that these advertisers resorted to broadcasting in order to disseminate their misleading and often fraudulent sales propaganda."

The advertisers were, in fact, taking so many liberties with freedom of speech on the air that in the spring of 1935 the Communications Commission decreed that the ether waves must be cleaned up. The citing of twenty-one stations [2] for the broadcasting of a program for Marmola was one of the first moves in the clean-up cam-

[2] Besides KNX, the 50,000-watt station operating on a clear channel, the stations ordered to show cause why their licenses should not be revoked were WBAP, WGAR, WBAL, WIOD, WJR, WHO, WOW, WSMB, WTMJ, WHEC, WKBW, WGR, WOWO, KFRC, KMBC, KMOX, WJAS, WIRE, WIND, WJJD.

paign. Marmola is a fat reducer against which the
Federal Trade Commission had proceeded in
1929. According to medical testimony, the product, which contains thyroid extract, is highly dangerous when used indiscriminately. Under the
provision of the Trade Commission Act, which
prohibits unfair methods of competition in interstate commerce, the Federal Trade Commission
issued a cease and desist order against the product. The case was finally appealed to the United
States Supreme Court, and in one of the most
famous rulings affecting consumers the highest
court of the land held that although the evidence
indicated that the product was dangerous, the
Federal Trade Commission had made no showing
of unfair competition and therefore had exceeded
its authority.[3] The backers of Marmola were deprived of any real enjoyment from their Pyrrhic
victory because the Post Office Department
slapped down a fraud order banning the distribution of the fat reducer by mail. Nevertheless, the
sale of the product continued through drugstores,

[3] In 1937, the Federal Trade Commission issued another cease
and desist order against Marmola in which it was again asserted
that the fat reducer contains ingredients imminently dangerous
to the health of the consumer.

and advertising appeared in many publications. Advertising on the air was different, said the Federal Communications Commission. Radio stations were licensed to operate "in the public interest," and to permit the advertising of a product against which the government had taken such vigorous action, the FCC declared, indicated that the broadcasting industry was forgetting its obligations.

A year and a half after the Communications Commission issued its show cause order, all twenty-one of the offending stations were back in the good graces of the Commission. None had been punished. The Washington correspondent of the *Christian Science Monitor* observed that "the Commission's attempt to drive home a sense of social responsibility upon radio stations for the programs they sponsor is admittedly handicapped by the immediate intercession of local congressmen, in behalf of any blacklisted station."

Both of the major networks, as well as the majority of the individual stations, now have regular departments whose duty it is to scan the advertising scripts "from the viewpoints of fairness to radio listeners." [4] At the end of its first year of operation, the NBC's Department of Continuity Acceptance reported that there had been a total of 560 violations of the networks' policies (checked of course before the programs went on the air) and that the most persistent violator was the cosmetic and toilet-goods industry. Janet MacRorie, head of the department, was also reported by *Variety* as saying (February 5, 1936) that "NBC was on the verge of putting dentifrice copy under stiff restrictions. Distributors of toothpaste and powders won't be permitted to make any claims that cannot stand the test of laboratory analysis."

But all this checking and double checking of radio scripts by the special censors of the broadcasting stations have not prevented some of their best customers from making deceptive statements. In August, 1936, General Mills, Inc. stipulated, according to the Federal Trade Commission news release, that in radio advertising of Wheaties it would desist from making statements that "any of the proceeds from the sale

[4] Report of NBC's Department of Continuity Acceptance for the Year 1935.

of Wheaties is used to defray the costs of an operation or medical attention for a fictitious person named in a broadcast, or that any such operation or medical attention is dependent upon the sale of Wheaties."

The broadcasts of the medicine men, however, offend the Federal Trade Commission most frequently. Typical of its actions are those against Allura, an eyewash advertised as a substitute for glasses, Nacor and Nacor Caps, a remedy for bronchitis and tonsilitis which the Commission found did not measure up to the claims made for it, and Sendol, a cold, headache and pain cure whose radio advertising especially peeved the Commission because it was ballyhooed as safe even for children. These actions of the Federal Trade Commission, like those of the Communications Commission, do not mean that the advertising of the products is banned from the air. So long as the medicine men and the others mind their manners, they can continue to broadcast.

There is the implied promise, in many of the trade announcements, that in the near by and by, radio will no longer be a medicine man's show.

In an analysis of the 1936–37 radio contracts, Sol Taishoff pointed out in *Broadcasting* that:

"More important to the industry as a whole is the fact that the influx of new accounts to radio is tending towards weeding out of undesirable ones. Laxative and medical accounts, while not disbarred under any laws, are still regarded generally as not in the best of taste. More than noticeable has been the pruning down of such accounts, particularly at peak times, and their replacement with business in the more desirable lines. . . . The Federal Communications Commission, whose reactions have been regarded as a barometer, has not cited a station for several months, so far as known, because of program complaints. A year ago, there were a dozen a week."

As the more desirable accounts (automobile, banks, gasoline refiners) come in, the medicine men may find that radio stations are less eager to sell them time. It will be a long, long while, however, before the manufacturers and distributors of nostrums find that there is no room on the air for their shows and ballyhoo. The average big station broadcasts for sixteen or more hours a day; if you divide sixteen hours into fifteen-minute periods, or even half-hour periods, and multiply this by 670, approximately the number of commercial stations as of January 1, 1937, you will see how many sponsors are needed before all the time available can be sold. In 1932, when the Federal Trade Commission issued its survey on "Commercial Radio Advertising," 63.86 percent of the total hours of broadcasting reported by the 582 stations were used for sustaining (non-commercial) programs. The gross receipts for the year (1931) were $77,758,048; for 1936, the indications are that the receipts will exceed $100,000,000. Considering, however, that many of the stations have raised their rates, it will be seen that there is ample time, now used for sustaining programs, still available for the nostrum vendors as well as for other business men and propagandists. In 1936, NBC announced that 71 percent of its programs were sustaining; only 29 percent sponsored.

There is no question but that the radio has given the medicine men's business a tremendous boost, and that the buying public, for whom the shows are put on, has been cheated both because of the exaggerated claims made for the products and their exorbitant price. But curbing the medicine men on the air is only a minor palliative. So long as the advertisers pay for the show, they can do far more than merely bamboozle the public.

The power wielded by the money man is well enough known. The radio stations must obey and please the Communications Commission; they must also satisfy the public, because only by proving that the unseen audience tunes in on their station can they sell their service. But the advertiser is the one who directly supplies the income, and his interests take precedence over those of the public.

In addition to the censorship that the stations exercise, the advertisers also wield a big blue pencil. The advertiser is, in fact, the first censor. His influence is only indirect on the programs sponsored by the stations, but for the programs which he arranges and pays for, he determines exactly what the public may and may not hear. In the past, there have been many complaints about the debasement of the public mind by the low level of the advertisers' shows; now, as the radio advertisers begin to make a quasi-intellectual appeal, the power they wield becomes a matter for more serious concern.

This type of control is exemplified by the exit of Alexander Woollcott from the Cream of Wheat program. Why the cereal processors hired Woollcott in the first place, why they thought the "sophisticated" ex-*New York World* and *New Yorker* columnist would increase the sale of a babies' gruel, is a mystery that can be explained only by one of radio's geniuses. In any event, Woollcott was hired, paid what he would probably describe as a "princely sum," and forthwith became one of the brightest stars in the radio world. His fans were many and devoted; presumably the Town Crier was fulfilling his part of the bargain and delivering the goods, or rather, selling them. But in November, 1935, his sponsors became restive.

In the course of his radio columning, the Town Crier had made many caustic remarks about Hitler and Mussolini. He had also discussed other subjects which the makers of Cream of Wheat were afraid might be offensive to certain large groups of customers. Woollcott was asked please to stop making such remarks. A few weeks later he was informed that unless he promised to keep mum on controversial subjects, or rather on subjects which his sponsors considered controversial, his broadcasts would be discontinued after December 29, even though his contract still had thirteen more weeks to run. Woollcott went off the air the last week of December. In an interview printed in the *Chicago Daily News* he explained:

"I could not in self respect guarantee to keep silent about Hitler, Mussolini or any other bully, jingo or lyncher. It would be unfair both to myself and my sponsor to try and continue under censorship, for the fact that taboos existed would lessen my own interest in the broadcasts and make them deteriorate in short order. . . .

"For the first two hours after I had made the great renunciation I felt very noble. I felt happy. I had won my own self esteem. I was preparing to be a hero. . . . Then I realized that the stand I had taken against censorship was nothing more than would have been made by any decent man with the courage of a diseased mouse. . . ."

Other radio advertisers saw their chance to capitalize on Woollcott's popularity, and immediately began to bid for his services. He refused all of the offers with the excuse that he was tired of the sound of his own voice. When the reporter for the *Daily News* inquired whether Woollcott believed the promises of complete freedom of speech made by his would-be sponsors, the Town Crier countered neatly. "I suspect," he said, "that none of the big national advertisers would be any more considerate and liberal than the one from whom I have just parted."

But broadcasting has its attractions. A year after the Town Crier went into retirement, he was again on the air. This time he was in the employ of Liggett & Myers. From advertising babies' pap he had graduated to plugging Granger Pipe Tobacco.

Some of the advertisers, especially those sponsoring news commentators, vigorously deny that their performers are influenced by business expediency. At a hearing before the Communications Commission in the summer of 1936, the Radio Corporation of America was charged with monopolistic control of the manufacture of radio receiving sets. Boake Carter, commentator for the Philco Radio and Television Corporation, repeated, as part of his regular news broadcast over the Columbia System, the speech attacking the RCA. Business relations between the RCA and Philco, one of its licensees, had been strained for some time before the speech, and shortly thereafter Philco instituted a suit against the Radio Corporation charging its agents with bribing a group of its girl employees, enmeshing them in compromising situations, and obtaining from them confidential information about Philco's business. But the business enmity existing between the two companies, said Philco, had nothing whatever to do with the remarks made by Carter. In a full-page advertisement in *Time,* Philco announced that when Boake Carter is on the air, his observations are "unhampered, untrammelled, uncensored . . . whether or not they agree with the listener or the sponsor. Five times a week Boake Carter expresses *his* [sic] opinions on any subject his news-sense deems important. No matter how controversial the topic . . . no matter whose toes may be trod upon . . . he is at liberty to voice his personal opinions and reactions . . . Philco's year-round expression of its belief that freedom of speech means freedom of the air as well as of the press. . . ."

Despite the special circumstances which

prompted this advertisement, the fact that Philco felt it necessary to make such assertions is a sad commentary on the state of freedom of speech, when the speaker is in the hire of the advertisers. Protestations that no censorship is exercised, always suggest that such censorship is practiced. The Woollcott incident gives point to such charges.

Every year sees changes in the radio programs acclaimed by the public. Newspapers run along pretty much the same from year to year, but the radio is no such humdrum matter. The entertainment offered must continually be varied. One year it is the variety show, another the "amateurs." Mrs. Franklin D. Roosevelt has been sponsored by the makers of Palmolive soap, Albert Spalding by Fletcher's Castoria, Drew Pearson and Robert Allen, authors of *The Nine Old Men* by the Gruen Watch Company and Warden Lawes of Sing Sing is featured by the Sloan Liniment Company while Heywood Broun does a radio column for the Pep Boys Auto Supplies. In their search for novelty, the advertisers have engaged the services even of that expert pantomimist, Harpo Marx.

The popularity of news broadcasts, radio columning, and editorializing is growing rapidly. The Henry Ford type of program is also increasing in popularity, both with the public and with the advertisers. In 1936–37 a group of bankers followed the lead of Ford and General Motors and combined little "talks" with the music of the Philadelphia Symphony Orchestra. Such programs are far more dangerous to the country's health than all the fifth-rate vaudeville which has been presented on the air. But so long as broadcasting is supported by business, our business rulers will be free to "entertain" the public in the way they think best.

VI

POLITICAL INTERFERENCE

O NE of the great American myths is that the operation of radio broadcasting for private profit assures the freedom of the air waves from political interference.

How this misconception ever achieved popular acceptance is hard to understand. For no one may operate a broadcasting station without a federal license and the party in power has always had a majority on the licensing commission.

The Radio Act of 1927 created a commission of five, no more than three of whom could be members of the same party. The Republicans were in office when the first appointments were made, and three of the five men were, of course, Republicans.

In the Communications Act of 1934, the number of commissioners was increased to seven and Section 4 (b) provides that "Not more than four commissioners shall be members of the same po-

litical party." The Democratic party was in office
when the original appointments were made, and
four of the commissioners are Democrats. In
paragraph *f* of the same section, the law also provides that "Four members of the Commission
shall constitute a quorum thereof." Thus it would
be possible for the party in office to rule the Commission absolutely.

Under the war emergency powers of the President, the act also provides:

"Upon proclamation by the President that there
exists war or a threat of war or a state of public peril or
disaster or other national emergency, or in order to
preserve the neutrality of the United States, the President may suspend or amend, for such time as he may
see fit, the rules and regulations applicable to any or all
stations within the jurisdiction of the United States as
prescribed by the Commission, and may cause the closing
of any station for radio communication." (Sec. 606-*c*)

During a state of war, the control of radio by
the government may be necessary. But who is to
define "a state of public peril . . . or other national emergency"? It may conceivably be a general strike in a single city, or in a certain section
of the country. The President need not take over

all radio stations but only those which reach listeners in the affected areas. Or, the emergency powers may be used to quiet political opposition. Without a more exact definition, we leave radio communication legally open to seizure by any President who aspires to dictatorship.

The power granted under this section is as great and as far-reaching as any that might be derived from President Roosevelt's plan, as his opponents describe it, to "pack" the Supreme Court by a rejuvenation process. But there was no public outcry nor any condemnation of the provision. It slipped into the radio law without any real opposition and without any reverent allusions to the constitution or its first amendment.

The section of the present law under which this power is granted is copied from the Radio Act of 1927. While this act was in force, the United States passed through a period which was described by the President as a "national emergency." We thus have an opportunity to examine how in practice, rather than merely in theory, this grant of power may be used.

On August 14, 1933, Harold A. Lafount, one

of the Federal Radio Commissioners, issued a statement to broadcasters that:

"It is the patriotic, if not the bounden and legal duty of all licensees of radio broadcasting stations to deny their facilities to advertisers who are disposed to defy, ignore, or modify the codes established by the N. R. A."

If this is not dictation by the party in power, what is? Officially, the President did not exercise his emergency power over radio communications, but through the Radio Commission, the presidential wish was made known. Certainly any similar attempt to control the press would have created a sensation. Not so with radio.

Even before the Commission issued its public statement, the National Broadcasting Company had established a policy of "coöperation" with the Administration. In May, 1933, Harold P. Redden of the American Legion broadcast from Station WBZA, which is owned by the Westinghouse Company and operated by the NBC. During the course of his speech, Mr. Redden made several critical remarks about the National Economy Act which had not been included in his submitted manuscript. The manager of the station immediately directed a letter to the American Legion in which he pointed out that:

". . . we are obliged to impose regulatory and prohibitory 'rules of the game.' These are prescribed by our editorial policy, customary among all broadcasting stations, and have their origin in regulations of the Federal Radio Commission.

"Particularly at a time of national crisis, we believe that any utterance on the radio that tends to disturb the public confidence in its President is a disservice to the people themselves and is hence inimical to the national welfare."

The Columbia Broadcasting .System was equally anxious to serve President and country. The American Alliance requested that WJSW of Washington, a station owned by CBS, broadcast a speech opposing recognition of Russia. Henry A. Bellows, then vice president of the Columbia network, and its "ambassador" at Washington, declared:

". . . no broadcast would be permitted over the Columbia Broadcasting System that in any way was critical of any policy of the Administration—that the Columbia system was at the disposal of President Roosevelt and his administration and they would permit no broadcast that did not have his approval. He was unusually frank in outlining the position of the Columbia system stating that he felt that President Roosevelt should be supported by the Columbia Broadcasting System whether right or wrong and that inasmuch as he had complete jurisdiction over the programs he was going to see to it that no criticism of any policy or proposed policy was made over the Columbia system." [1]

Two years later, Mr. Bellows, writing in *Harper's Magazine*, attempted to prove that no censorship by or on behalf of the Administration existed because no one had testified to it at a special hearing of the Communications Commission. Quite conceivably the reason may have been similar to that stated by D. W. May in 1928 to the members of the Interstate Commerce Commission:

"Mr. May— . . . Answering Senator Hawes' question as to why more broadcasters did not appear. I happened to meet a total of four broadcasters around my city since I was here at the last hearing. I said to each one of them: 'My God, why don't you go down and tell what you think of the radio situation?' The response in each case was, 'Why should I go down and risk losing my wave length and my station?' "

[1] Letter from Walter C. Reynolds, secretary of the American Alliance, to Senator Arthur R. Robinson of Indiana.

It is Mr. Bellows' contention that the Republicans kept themselves off the air. "The general attitude," he writes, "was expressed by a minority senator on my urgent invitation to discuss the banking measures. 'No,' he said, 'I'd rather wait till I can do it without being suspected of high treason.' " [2]

Mr. Bellows does admit that "in a few instances, however, partly in the hope of currying favor, and partly misled by an excess of zeal based on the oft-repeated statement that we were in the midst of an emergency comparable to that of war, individual stations did in those first few months of the New Deal refuse facilities to its critics." This, he comments, was an error of judgment.

In a series of articles on censorship published in June, 1934, the *New York Herald Tribune* reported other instances of how the Republican party, for which it is one of the most potent mouthpieces, was kept off the air. During the first three years of the Radio Forum conducted by the *Washington (D. C.) Star,* the director of the forum estimated that there were an equal number

[2] "Is Radio Censored?", November, 1935.

of Republican and Democratic speakers. "But in the last sixty weeks," the *Herald Tribune* complained, "only half a dozen Republicans have been among the five dozen invited speakers."

Even though the political bias of the *Herald Tribune* must be taken into consideration, the evidence presented is significant. During the first days of the New Deal when General Johnson was whooping it up for the Blue Eagle, and President Roosevelt was reporting so persuasively in his fireside chats on the state of the union, the opposition was strangely silent. In the days of the "emergency" members of the opposition discovered that their value as radio performers was considered nil by the broadcasting companies.

The Republicans, of course, are in a poor position to complain, for the present radio law was developed under Republican sponsorship. While Herbert Hoover, that rugged individualist and ardent advocate of self-government in business, was Secretary of Commerce, he pressed upon Congress the importance of adequate government regulation of radio. Under the Radio Act of 1912, all operators of wireless transmitters were required to secure a federal license. It was

a "safety at sea" measure and since the regulation
of shipping is one of the functions of the Department of Commerce, it was entrusted with the
administration of the law and the issuing of licenses.

The draftsmen of the first radio act were not
visionaries; they did not foresee the advent of
popular broadcasting. But when popular broadcasting began, the new industry was governed by
the provisions of the old law.

The demand for broadcasting licenses soon
created problems which the legislative draftsmen
had not contemplated. No limitation had been
placed on the number of licenses which might be
issued; but there is a limited number of wave
lengths available in the broadcast band. The Secretary of Commerce issued licenses so long as
there were wave lengths on which radio stations
could operate. When no more were available, he
refused to grant broadcasting licenses. This, the
courts held, was exceeding his authority. The
Secretary of Commerce was obliged to issue
licenses whether or not there was room on the
air. Three years later, in 1926, the courts ruled in
another test case that the Secretary of Commerce

had no authority to restrict the wave length, transmitting power, or hours of operation of a radio station, or to limit the terms of licenses. It was apparent that if the government was to keep order on the air, a new law was needed.

The Radio Act of 1927 was approved nine days before the expiration of the Sixty-ninth Congress. Because of a filibuster, the appropriation bill containing an item for the Commission did not pass. The new Commission therefore had to ask alms of the Department of Commerce, which donated $28,313 for the remainder of the fiscal year. This sum was insufficient to pay the salaries of the commissioners or of an adequate clerical staff. For the fiscal year 1937, Congress appropriated $1,474,000 for the Communications Commission.

In accordance with the act, the country was divided into five zones, and one commissioner was appointed from each zone. This system laid the foundation for complaints of favoritism and sectionalism. Each commissioner, it was charged, was jealous of the privileges granted his constituents, and if he forgot his obligations in considering the general good, he was reminded of them by the congressmen from his zone. "Probably no quasi-judicial body was ever subjected to so much congressional pressure as the Federal Radio Commission," wrote Lawrence F. Schmeckebier, "and much of this came at a time when a majority of the Commission had not been confirmed." [3] The Davis Amendment of 1928, which provided for the allocation of broadcasting licenses equally to each zone and fairly and equitably to the states within each zone in proportion to population, was an attempt to correct this situation. It proved a complete failure and was repealed in the spring of 1936.

The first set of Radio Commissioners entrusted with the licensing function, with the power to assign wave lengths and to determine whether stations were operating "in the public interest," were perhaps no worse, but certainly they were no better than the usual political appointees. From the first zone, there was Orestes H. Caldwell, an engineer, formerly editor of *Radio Retailing,* one of the McGraw-Hill publications. At the hearing for the confirmation of his ap-

[3] *The Federal Radio Commission—Its History—Activities and Organization,* Brookings Institution, 1932.

pointment, Mr. Caldwell testified that while he was serving as a government employee, he was receiving a $7,000 yearly retainer from McGraw-Hill. Because his confirmation had been delayed, McGraw-Hill also lent Mr. Caldwell $833 a month pending the payment of his government salary. The Senate confirmed the Caldwell appointment by a margin of one vote.

Rear Admiral W. H. G. Bullard was the commissioner from the second zone. Even though death cut short his radio service (he died in November, 1927), his name would still have gone down in radio history. According to the story told by Owen D. Young, Admiral Bullard was the bearer of a message from President Wilson requesting that the General Electric Company should not sell the rights to the Alexanderson alternator to foreigners, the message which is supposed to have inspired the organization of the Radio Corporation of America. By the time he was appointed to the Radio Commission, Admiral Bullard knew considerably more about the RCA than he did when he went to Mr. Young merely as a messenger boy. During the days when the RCA was being organized, he diligently strove to obtain the official approval of the Navy for the formation of the new trust. Even though he was unsuccessful in this, the RCA directors were glad when, at their request that President Wilson designate an official observer to sit at the Board meetings, the Admiral was the man chosen. Of Admiral Bullard's career in radio the Sirovich Committee observes:

"The motives of Admiral Bullard appear from this record conclusively to have been personal rather than official, for the record establishes that Admiral Bullard had an ambition to resign from the Navy to become head of the Radio Corporation of America." [4]

This ambition was never realized.

From the third zone there was Judge Eugene O. Sykes, the only member of the original group who now is a member of the Communications Commission. Before his appointment, Judge Sykes was a member of the Mississippi Supreme Court Bench.

Henry A. Bellows was the commissioner from the fourth zone. He had been manager of station

[4] Appendix to Hearings Before the Commission on Patents, House of Representatives, in HR 4523, Part IV, page 3397.

WCCO of Minneapolis before his appointment and was the only one of the commissioners who had had any practical experience in broadcasting. The more cogent reason for his appointment was the excellent coöperation he had given Secretary Hoover in securing the passage of the Radio Act. Commissioner Bellows resigned after eight months, still unconfirmed and drawing no pay, but the time he had given to the Commission was not entirely wasted, for in 1930 he became vice president of the Columbia Broadcasting System.

The fifth member of the Commission, Col. John F. Dillon of San Francisco, died a few months after the Radio Commission was formed.

The Radio Act originally provided that after one year the Commission was to become an appellate body, and with the exception of its power to revoke licenses, all of its other authority and duties were to revert to the Secretary of Commerce. But at the end of the first year, the Radio Commission had barely made a start on the work to be done, and Congress voted that it should continue on probation for another twelve months. In 1929, the life of the Commission was extended for still another year, but not before the Congressional committees had taken evidence from operators of radio stations and from the commissioners, too, as to how the Commission had handled radio affairs. Throughout the testimony there is reference to favoritism shown by the Commission to the two major chains. In 1930, President Hoover recommended that the Commission be made a permanent body. No longer would it have to report annually to Congress.

The Senate, however, has continued to cross-examine nominees for the Radio Commission before confirming the President's appointments. Among other things, these Senate hearings give a clear-cut picture of the way in which the Commission has been used to solve the patronage problem. There is, for example, the testimony given by Thad H. Brown in 1932. Mr. Brown is now one of the seven members of the Federal Communications Commission.

The chairman at the hearing was probably overstating the case when he said that "there is no politician now on the Commission in the same sense that Mr. Brown is." Both before and since, appointments to the Commission have been determined by politics. The political tie-up was particularly easy to trace, however, in this case. Thad Brown had been President Hoover's campaign manager in Ohio, and it was in a letter to Brown that Mr. Hoover announced his candidacy for the presidency. Mr. Brown was one of the key men of the Ohio Republican party, and had held state offices for many years. During the time that he was Secretary of State of Ohio there was a scandal about losses of money resulting from unnecessary delay by collectors in depositing funds paid for automobile licenses. After the attorney general had ruled that the Secretary of State as well as a group of bankers were responsible, a committee of the bankers headed by the vice president of the Guardian Trust Co. collected and turned in to the state more than fifty thousand dollars. Mr. Brown testified that he did not contribute a cent to the fund.

Originally he had hoped to be one of the first radio commissioners, but the appointment from the second zone went to Admiral Bullard. A year after Mr. Hoover took office, his services to the party were recognized by his appointment as counsel to the Federal Power Commission. Six months later, he became counsel to the Radio Commission.

While he was acting in this capacity, the renewal of the licenses of the broadcasting stations controlled by the Radio Corporation of America through its subsidiary, the National Broadcasting Company, was before the Commission. The district court of Delaware had ruled that the "tying clause" in the licenses issued by the RCA to manufacturers of receiving sets was in restraint of trade. This clause required that the licensed manufacturers use only RCA to make their sets initially operative. In the Radio Act, and there is a similar provision in the Communications Act, "The licensing authority is . . . directed to refuse a station license . . . to any person, firm, company, or corporation, or any subsidiary thereof, which has been finally adjudged guilty by a Federal Court of unlawfully monopolizing or attempting unlawfully to monopolize . . . radio communication directly or indirectly, through the control of the manufacture or sale of radio apparatus. . . ." Mr. Brown testified before the senate committee that he believed the section applied to the judgment of the district court and "that if there was any doubt in the minds of the members of the Commission about it, I thought that doubt should be resolved in favor of the public." The legal opinion of its counsel apparently did not jibe with the opinion of the Commission because when the case came up for hearing Mr. Brown was on leave of absence granted by the chairman of the Commission. The renewal of the licenses was approved.[5]

Charges that the President was paying political debts have frequently been made after the naming of radio commissioners. When James H. Hanley was appointed commissioner succeeding C. McK. Saltzman, Washington gossipers remembered that Hanley had been vice president of the Nebraska Democratic State Committee and a co-worker of Arthur Mullen, Roosevelt's floor manager at the 1932 Chicago convention. Soon after Hanley was appointed, Mullen began to practice law in Washington, and it was

[5] According to E. Pendleton Herring, in the *Harvard Business Review* (January, 1935), the vote was 3 to 2. The Commission decided that inasmuch as the monopolistic practices related to radio apparatus and not to broadcasting, they had no power to deny the renewals of the licenses. There were immediate protests that the Commission was under the thumb of the RCA.

reported that Mullen was a lobbyist for the RCA.[6]

Additional evidence of the usefulness of the Commission to the party in power was indicated when Herbert L. Pettey was named Secretary of the Commission. Pettey had been in charge of radio during President Roosevelt's 1932 campaign, and apparently he continued to handle radio matters for the Democratic National Committee after he was drawing his salary from the federal government. On September 12, 1933, Postmaster James A. Farley wrote to Pettey:

"In order to prevent misunderstanding in the future I have advised the broadcasting stations that the only person authorized to represent me on radio matters is Mr. Herbert L. Pettey who was in charge of radio for us during the last campaign.

"Any person wishing radio time should clear his request through Richard F. Roper, the executive secretary of the Democratic National Committee, who is the only person authorized to take up such a matter with Mr. Pettey for the Committee.

"I think it is very important that matters of this kind be handled in an orderly way."

6 *New York Herald-Tribune,* June, 1934.

Mr. Pettey did not consider the letter at all embarrassing, and when Senator Vandenberg (Republican) asked whether Pettey solicited free time from the broadcasting companies, Pettey sent him a copy of the letter. Presumably it was to be no secret that the party in power put one of its men into the Commission to serve it. A few months before President Roosevelt began his second campaign, Pettey resigned from his government post and became assistant manager of station WHN of New York, owned by the Loew interests.

The present seven commissioners are Chairman Anning S. Prall, Eugene O. Sykes, Thad Brown, Paul A. Walker, Dr. Irvin Stewart, Norman S. Case and George H. Payne.

The Microphone ("original United States Radio Newspaper") supplies the following information about the commissioners.

"Head of this body is Chairman Anning S. Prall of New York, a man of charming personality with experience in government, and with a thorough schooling in the art of politics. . . . He has one of the best radio voices. He probably could make a topnotch announcer.

As chairman he has fought to retain the commercial system of radio in all of its present aspects.

"Judge Eugene O. Sykes from Mississippi, is chairman of the Commission's broadcast division. . . . For a year he served as chairman of the FCC but his penchant for politics . . . and backing the wrong horse . . . cost him the job. . . . He too is strong for the commercial system of radio.

"Vice Chairman of the broadcast division is Norman S. Case, former governor of Rhode Island, enthusiastic National Guard Cavalry officer, peacemaker. . . . He attracted President Roosevelt's attention during a Governors' conference called by former President Hoover . . . which was supposed to solve the depression. . . . A conservative Republican. . . . He wants the Commission to work harmoniously.

"Commissioner Thad Brown has been in politics all his life. . . . Depend on Brown to pursue a middle of the road course.

"Irvin Stewart, youngest member of the Commission . . . doesn't hanker for fights but gets into them because he sticks to his convictions. . . .

"Paul Atlee Walker, who is conducting the A.T. and T. investigation, has his own opinions about radio. . . . Walker made his reputation as chairman of the Oklahoma Corporation Commission which regulates utilities. Regulating rates means to him that they should be regulated downward. He became known as a liberal

among utility commissioners and it was because of this
that President Roosevelt picked him for the FCC.

"George H. Payne is earning the sobriquet of the
'people's radio man'. . . . He was a progressive Republican for years. Payne thinks that radio can be
made a valuable educational medium. He has told broadcasters bluntly that if they don't look forward and give
the people worthwhile programs, the people will demand
that the government provide them." [7]

When George H. Payne's term expired in the
spring of 1936, there was considerable specula-
tion whether President Roosevelt would re-
nominate him. According to *Variety,* leading
Democratic politicians urged the President to
"ditch" Payne, and to choose a Republican "who
would work more harmoniously with administration members of the Commission." The reap-
pointment, it reported, came after a delegation
of thirty members of the Senate, including pro-
gressives of both parties, had called at the White
House.

Commissioner Payne's outspoken criticism of
his fellow commissioners has for years been caus-
ing embarrassment and ill feelings at the Wash-

[7] August 28, 1936.

ington headquarters. In an address delivered at Harvard University (January 13, 1936) he told his audience: "The Commission is young and still has its growing pains. Not infrequently, I believe, when I am not around, I am referred to as one of the distinct ones."

The family squabbling and the washing of the Commission's dirty linen in public is, of course, undignified, but it has the marked advantage of giving the public an insight into the functioning of the government's radio czars. To an audience gathered at Cornell University, Commissioner Payne declared:

"In this country the political activity of broadcasters is a regrettable fact. It would be unfair to place the entire responsibility for the situation on them, for in the early days of chaos possibly it seemed to them the only way of obtaining what they considered their rights. . . . In the year the present Commission has been in existence there has been a decided improvement, I sincerely believe; although someone has said that, even now, you cannot come out of an office in the Communications Commission without stepping on one or two broadcast lawyers." [8]

[8] August 21, 1935.

Again, in his Harvard address, Commissioner Payne lambasted the commercial broadcasters and his fellow commissioners.

"The most important of the many problems that have confronted the Federal Communications Commission in the year and a half of its existence, has been that of combatting the impression that the new Commission was or could be dominated by the bodies, industries or corporations over which it was given by Congress the power of regulation. There was a belief that our predecessor, the old Radio Commission, was dominated by the industry that it was supposed to restrain and control. I am very happy to say that *such is not now the case* [italics mine] and that many of the corporations over which we have jurisdiction are quite convinced that the Commission or those divisions with which they deal form independent judgments without bias or without prejudice and with no other interest or consideration than regard for their oath of office."

Besides all the political scandals, there have been other attacks on the integrity of the government's appointed censors. The most serious of these was the Willard incident. Two New York State companies had applications before the Commission: WNBF of Binghamton for permission to increase its transmitting power, and the Knox Gelatin Co. for a permit to establish a new station. Because of natural limitations, only one of the applications could be granted. A. Mortimer Prall, son of the Commission's chairman, and Major Malcolm M. Kilduff were in a room in the Willard Hotel after the hearings on the applications. The adjoining room was occupied by persons who discussed the applications in loud voices and, according to statements made by A. Mortimer Prall, mention was made of $25,000 which could be used to "fix" the case. The incident was immediately reported to Commissioner Prall, who asked the Department of Justice to investigate. After he had been told that it was apparently an "irresponsible" conversation, the FCC decided to investigate for itself. Six months later the Commission made public its findings, and those of the Department of Justice. The occupants of the room in which the conversation was alleged to have taken place were Cecil D. Mastin, manager of WNBF; Harold E. Smith, manager of WOKO, Albany; Alfons B. Landa, Washington attorney for WNBF; and Maurice Jansky, a radio engineer.

Some of the interesting angles that came to

light were that hearings on the Knox application were speeded up at the request of the Broadcasting Division and the chairman's office; that the Knox group was listed in a telephone directory as a broadcasting station before the application for permission to build a transmitter had been filed, and that the examiners who had heard the Knox application "might have read" the unfavorable report on WNBF before writing a favorable one on the Knox application. The engineering division of the Commission had made an adverse recommendation on this application which the Examiner, P. W. Seward, disregarded. The name of Senator Robert Wagner was also brought into the matter by Chairman Prall who told Harry Butcher, Washington manager of the Columbia Broadcasting System, and one of its vice presidents, that the Knox group had originally been recommended to him in a letter from the senator.

For a long time there were rumors that Senator Wheeler, chairman of the Interstate Commerce Commission, was going to call for an investigation of the FCC. But nothing came of it. The Willard matter was officially closed in May of 1936 when the Commission denied the applications of both stations.

But this did not end the Willard incident. In October, still another application was filed for the channel which had already caused so much trouble. The new applicant was the Citizens Broadcasting Company in which the Transamerican Broadcasting & Television Corporation is financially interested. The buzzing in Washington started all over, when it was discovered that A. Mortimer Prall was an employee of Transamerican. He was hired shortly before the application for the wave length was filed, but resigned before it came up for hearing. Charges of bias and favoritism have frequently been made against the Commission; *l'affaire* Willard gave the muckrakers some of their meatiest gossip.

VII

STAR CHAMBER PROCEEDINGS

"Nothing in this Act shall be understood or construed to give the Commission the power of censorship over the radio communications or signals transmitted by any radio station, and no regulation or condition shall be promulgated or fixed by the Commission which shall interfere with the right of free speech by means of radio communication. No person within the jurisdiction of the United States shall utter any obscene, indecent or profane language by means of radio communications." Sec. 326, Communications Act of 1934; originally Sec. 29, Radio Act of 1927.

OF ALL the jokers written by our lawmakers, there is none which can rank with the prohibition against censorship by the federal radio authority. The section is unequivocal, explicit and apparently susceptible of no interpretation other than the one intended.

But in the ten years that the radio laws have been in effect, the broadcasting industry and the public have had ample opportunity to observe how one paragraph in a legal document can nullify another. The radio commissioners were expressly forbidden to censor; they were, however, ordered to issue licenses upon findings that the "public interest, convenience, or necessity" would be served. It is on the authority of these five words that the radio commissioners have based their right to exert a direct and positive censorship over broadcasting.

This interpretation of the duty imposed on the Commission was publicly stated by Henry A. Bellows in a speech before the League of Women Voters, two months after the radio commissioners assumed office.

"We are to determine who shall and who shall not broadcast and how such broadcasting shall be carried on simply in accordance with our conception of public interest, convenience and necessity. It is an appalling responsibility. The law tells us that we shall have no right of censorship over radio programs but the physical facts of radio transmission compel what is in effect a censorship of the most extraordinary kind."

This frank speech had the approval of the other four commissioners. It was included in their first annual report, and can therefore be accepted as the point of view, not of one man but of the commissioners as a group. From the very beginning the commissioners have disagreed about many things but there never was any real argument about their right to determine what should and should not be broadcast.

Mr. Bellows now admits to some pangs of conscience when contemplating the precedents of censorship which he, and the other first commissioners, established. He terms the practice of taking into account the type and quality of programs when a station's license came up for renewal "a flagrant violation of the very law we were appointed to administer." [1] He mentions the mitigating circumstances: the chaos which existed in broadcasting; the meekness with which the industry and its legal advisers submitted to the omniscience of the Commission, and the court rulings which upheld the Commission's broad interpretation of its powers. Unfortunately, Bellows' hindsight is better than his foresight.

History proves conclusively that a government, or its agent, does not easily surrender power. Either a new law or an amendment of the present one is needed if the Commission is to be-

[1] *Harper's Magazine,* November, 1935,

come, as the legislators presumably meant it to
be, merely the policeman of the air waves. This
may be achieved sooner than even the most op-
timistic believe possible, because of the growing
tyranny of the Communications Commission.

Rule No. 177 issued in the spring of 1936
marked a new high in the Commission's arroga-
tion of authority. The order specified that no
American station could rebroadcast a foreign
program without the written permission of the
Federal Communications Commission except—
and the exception was as amazing as the order
itself—if the program was transmitted entirely,
or almost entirely, by telephone. As *The Nation*
pointed out at the time, this was not only a direct
subsidy to the telephone company but favored
the big stations, which regularly use the telephone
wires, over the small ones which pick up foreign
programs from the short waves. Yet this show
of favoritism was not nearly so important as the
outright declaration of the Commission that it
intended to censor what the American public
might hear. The next step obviously might have
been direct and open censorship of programs
manufactured in America for domestic consump-

tion. The rule was to have gone into force on July 1, but so loud and pointed were the protests that the Commission made a hasty retreat. It rewrote Rule 177, omitting the paragraph establishing FCC censorship of foreign programs. Its attempted usurpation of power was a fiasco, but the Commission may try again.

When the Federal Communications Commission took over the duties and responsibilities of the old radio commission, it had a well-established precedent of censorship by what Louis G. Caldwell, who was the first General Counsel of the Federal Radio Commission, terms "subsequent punishment." If the programs which had been broadcast by a station did not please the Commission, its operator could simply be put out of business by a refusal to renew his license. This interpretation and practical application of the "public interest, convenience or necessity" clause has been upheld by the Court of Appeals of the District of Columbia in the famous Brinkley case in which the court quoted Matthew IV that "by their fruits shall ye know them."

Both before and since this decision the radio commissioners have not only actively applied the power of censorship granted them under their licensing authority, but they have availed themselves of every means to increase that power. In the radio laws of 1927 and 1934 it was provided that licenses to broadcasters be issued for not "longer than three years." At first the Commission issued broadcasting licenses for ninety-day periods. This policy was defended on the grounds that the short-term licenses facilitated the reallocation of wave lengths and thus simplified the task of creating order on the air. But long after the Commission had completed its policeman's job, the short-term licenses were continued. Even today, with the broadcasting industry well organized and comparatively well behaved, the Commission issues licenses which must be renewed every six months. The short-term license is a potent device for control which the Commission is unwilling to surrender.

In 1936, the Commission sought to increase its power by suggesting to Congress the advisability of an amendment permitting it to suspend a station for bad programming. The Commission, of course, can revoke a license. For lesser offenses, Chairman Prall thought that suspension for a week, ten days or a month would be enough to take care of violators. It would be indeed. Close down a radio station for a week, and it would probably be forced out of business. Thus far, Congress has not indicated that it will grant Chairman Prall's request.

At present then, the Commission derives its power from the licensing function which includes the power to allot desirable or undesirable wave lengths, to permit an increase or order a decrease of transmitting power, and, by no means the last in importance, to approve or disapprove every sale or transfer of broadcasting facilities.

This last provision was supposed to prevent trafficking in broadcast licenses. Since the radio commission early recognized the right of priority, it has obviously been more advantageous to buy old equipment—and licenses—instead of applying to the Commission for a permit to establish a new station. These licenses may be worth tremendous sums; in 1936 the Columbia Broadcasting System contracted to pay $1,250,000 for KNX of Los Angeles, one of the most powerful stations on the West Coast, but at the time still on the Commission's blacklist because it had broadcast some forty odd medical programs to which the government's censors objected. There was considerable speculation as to the Commission's reaction to the deal. It was unhesitatingly approved. The licensing authority found that although the value of the KNX transmitting equipment was only $63,763.30, "it appears that consideration should be given to the earning power of such an investment as well as the fact that a very large listening public in the Western area will receive the Columbia service, where it has not heretofore been available." In other words, the FCC license was worth $1,186,236 or eighteen times as much as the equipment. This did not shock the FCC, which always passes on the reasonableness of prices, because the return on the CBS investment, it was found, would be approximately 16 or 17 percent, which the Commission considered good enough to merit Columbia's contract for a cool million and a quarter dollars. In approving the sale, the Commission also took the opportunity to declare a policy of encouraging competition between the networks, and to pat Columbia on the back. In reporting the Commission's blessing on the KNX deal, *Variety* commented:

"Radio attorneys generally were surprised at the way the broadcast czars smiled on CBS and flaggergasted that the commish went so far in declaring its belief that inter-web rivalry should be encouraged."

The only major business decision which operators of broadcasting stations may now make without asking the approval of the FCC is the fixing of the price at which they sell time on the air, and it has been frequently proposed that, like railroads and other public utilities, these rates should also be determined by the government.

So far, every increase in authority has been used by the radio commissioners to harass small stations and minority groups. The Davis Amendment, included in the act of March 28, 1928, which granted the Federal Radio Commission a second year of life, directed the Commission to make a more equitable distribution of broadcasting licenses among the several sections of the country. The amendment was a direct answer to the complaints that the Commission was favoring certain groups and sections over others. The

Davis Amendment did not remedy this situation. But as a result of the legislative command, the Radio Commission undertook to redistribute broadcasting licenses and as a first step issued its famous Order 32 in which a group of stations was required to make a showing that their continued operation would serve public interest, convenience and necessity. One of the stations listed was WEVD, the Socialist station operated by the Debs Memorial Fund. Protests were immediately made that the Commission was attempting to delete a meritorious station because of its social and economic viewpoint. In the brief submitted by the station it was pointed out that:

"This station exists for the purpose of maintaining at least one channel of the air free and open to the uses of the workers. We admit without any apology that this station has no deep concern with reporting polo matches, or even giving instructions in how to play bridge and other classy games of chance. We are not convinced that the public necessity dictates the broadcasting of descriptions of ladies' fancy dresses at receptions in Fifth Avenue ball rooms. Unless the Commission discriminates against labor we intend to carry on with the purposes for which we were organized—a service to labor. . . . If WEVD is taken off the air and in fact if it is not treated on a parity with others who are richer and more influential with the government, the people of the nation can truly recognize that radio which might be such a splendid force for the honest clash of ideas,—creating a free market for thought,—is nothing but a tool to be used by the powerful against any form of disagreement, or any species of protest."

The license was renewed, and WEVD is still broadcasting—on an undesirable wave length. But in refuting the charges that had been made against it, the Commission made several interesting comments, which show the criterion used in determining whether a station is to be permitted to operate.

"Undoubtedly some of the doctrines broadcast over the station would not meet the approval of individual members of the Commission. . . . The Commission will not draw the line on any station doing an altruistic work, or which is the mouthpiece of a substantial political or religious minority. Such a station must, of course, comply with the requirements of the law and must be conducted with due regard for the opinion of others."

Superficially, this final statement appears fair enough. Certainly a station must abide by the law, but an interpretation by the Commission of whether or not a station is "conducted with due regard for the opinion of others" leaves a wide enough loophole for any censorship which the Commission may wish to exercise. The ruling in the WEVD case was, however, a useful and convenient one on which the Commission could rely when critics objected that it was favoring the air monopolists over the "little fellow." The Commission also sought comfort, and protection from the attacks of critics, because of its broadmindedness in regard to station WIBA partly owned by a newspaper which was the spokesman for the LaFollette progressive movement. According to the commissioners' statement, there had been considerable complaint about the quality of the programs of WIBA; still the license was renewed—*q.e.d.,* the charges that the Commission was attempting to silence minority groups was unfounded.

The Commission could not take equal satisfaction from its ruling on the application of WCFL operated by the Chicago Federation of Labor, for a modification of its license. WCFL was permitted to broadcast only until six in the evening, and in applying for a permit to operate during the evening hours, it pointed out that this was the only time when it could reach its real radio audience, since most of its listeners (that was in 1928) were at work during the day. Together with its application, WCFL sent petitions and letters from listeners. The Commission observed that the petitions were in mimeographed form, and that anyone can get signatures to a petition. It refused the request on the grounds that "there are not enough frequencies within the broadcast band to give to each of the various groups of persons in the United States a channel on which to operate a broadcasting station." This decision was appealed to the courts which upheld the Commission's ruling with the explanation that "meritorious stations should not be deprived of privileges merely to make room for another station inasmuch as such an attitude would greatly impair the cause of independent broadcasting."

The spokesman for the labor station next appealed directly to the legislators. A new law for the regulation of radio was being drafted (the White-Dill bill of 1930 for the establishment of a Communications Commission), and to the men who were attempting to devise a better way of controlling the radio, the representative of WCFL told how labor had been badgered and discriminated against. During his discourse, he remarked that the licensees of the best radio frequencies were "so influential that I doubt that Congress will dare to meet the situation."

Senator Glenn of Illinois, in whose state the labor station is located, proved sympathetic to the plight of his constituents, and an amendment to the White-Dill bill provided that a clear channel with power equal to the maximum permitted any station be assigned to labor. In the opinion of the radio committee of the American Bar Association, "It was only because of opposition to this and one or two other features of the bill in the House that the bill escaped becoming the law." Some time afterwards, labor agreed to compromise and instead of the clear channel which it had requested, it was authorized to increase the transmitting power of WCFL and to operate full time on the old frequency. WCFL now shares a clear channel, and the station operates as a member of the NBC Red and Blue networks.

In the same annual report in which the Commission stated the reasons for its original decision on the WCFL application, it reiterated and amplified its position in its decision on the applications of Great Lakes Broadcasting Co., Wilbur Glenn Voliva and Agriculture Broadcasting Co. At the time, Great Lakes Broadcasting Co. was controlled by the Commonwealth Edison Co., an Insull property. Voliva represented the House of David, a sect well known to baseball enthusiasts because all of the members of its team wear long beards. In denying his application for a broadcasting license, the Commission wrote:

"Propaganda stations (a term which is used here for the sake of convenience and not in a derogatory sense) are not consistent with the most beneficial sort of discussion of public questions. . . . If the question were now raised for the first time, after the Commission has given careful study to it, the Commission would not license any propaganda station, at least to an exclusive position on a cleared channel. . . . While the Commission is of the opinion that a broadcasting station engaged in general public service has, ordinarily, a claim to preference over a propaganda station it will apply this principle as to existing stations by giving preferential facilities to the former and assigning less desirable positions to the latter to the extent that engineering principles permit."

It was unfortunate that such a significant declaration should have been made in a matter in which one of the principles, because of the peculiarities of his sect, was something of a comic figure. The same rule, of course, applied to labor.

As E. Pendleton Herring pointed out in the *Harvard Business Review*: [2]

". . . the point seems clear that the Federal Radio Commission has interpreted the concept of public interest so as to favor in actual practice one particular group. While talking in terms of the public interest, convenience and necessity the Commission actually chose to further the ends of the commercial broadcasters. . . . underlying all considerations is the necessity of eliminating any element that might lessen the usefulness of the station as a device for attracting the buying public."

In three of its most important decisions, there have been mitigating circumstances which have taken the sting out of the Commission's rulings. Yet under cover of the "mitigating circumstances," the Commission used these cases to

[2] January, 1935.

establish its censorship power. When Dr. J. R. Brinkley, owner of station KFKB, was denied a renewal of his broadcasting license, he argued that this amounted to censorship. The Commission based its decision on the finding that Dr. Brinkley's broadcasting was not in the public interest because he used his station to advertise the Brinkley hospital and medicines. The question might logically be raised why it is any more reprehensible for a purveyor of patent medicines to use his own station to advertise his wares than it is for competitors to buy time from the commercial stations. In any event, the Commission did not like the programs that KFKB had broadcast, and it ruled that Dr. Brinkley must go off the air. The court upheld the decision, saying that "the Commission has merely exercised its undoubted right to take note of appellant's past conduct which is not censorship." It also repeated the rule expressed by the Commission in the Voliva case. "Obviously," it wrote, "there is no room in the broadcast band for every business or school of thought."

The real issues in the Norman Baker and the Rev. Robert P. Shuler cases, which along with the Brinkley decision stand as milestones in the history of censorship by the government, were also confused because both of the men, in addition to their crusading, could be charged with other offenses.

In 1928 Norman Baker, then owner of station KTNT (the last three letters inspired many a senatorial quip), testified before the Committee on Interstate Commerce that he had incurred the animosity of the utilities by permitting Senator Brookhart to carry on his campaign over KTNT; that the vested interests were further angered by the election of State Senator Ralph U. Thompson, an independent, from Baker's senatorial district; and that the wrath of other powerful interests was aroused because State Senator Kromme had been permitted to deliver an address over KTNT charging corruption in the Iowa State University. For these offenses, Baker complained, the wave length of his station had been changed, and when KTNT's license came up for renewal, the Commission decided that he should go off the air. In its decision, however, it also took cognizance of Baker's crusading, saying:

"The programs broadcast by Station KTNT have included personal and bitter attacks upon individuals, companies and associations, and whether warranted or unwarranted, such programs have not been in the public interest, convenience or necessity. This commission holds no brief for the Medical Associations and other parties whom Mr. Baker does not like. Their alleged sins may be at times of public importance, to be called to the attention of the public over the air in the right way. It shows that he continually and erratically over the air rides a personal hobby, his cancer cure ideas and his likes and dislikes of certain persons and things."

No one can object to the Commission's restriction on cancer-cure advertising. An adequate Food and Drug Act would take all such advertising off the air—and out of the newspapers and magazines. But the cancer cure happened to afford a convenient opportunity to establish a taboo on crusading. The lack of journalistic vigor characteristic of broadcast comment can in no small part be traced to this decision and to that in the Shuler case.

The Rev. Robert P. Shuler, pastor of Trinity Church, Los Angeles, operated KGEF, a noncommercial station whose facilities were lent to the Christian Missionary Alliance, the Los An-

geles Pacific College, the Volunteers of America
and others; but "Bob" Shuler saved enough time
on the air for his own crusading. It was to these
speeches that the Commission objected when
denying the renewal of his license. It declared
that:

". . . he has vigorously attacked by name all organizations, political parties, public officials, and individuals whom he has conceived to be moral enemies
of society or foes of the proper enforcement of the law.
He has believed it his duty to denounce by name any
enterprise, organization, or individual he personally
thinks is dishonest or untrustworthy. Shuler testified
that it was his purpose 'to try to make it hard for the
bad man to do wrong in the community.' "

This avowed purpose would seem to merit
praise, not censure. The Commission took the
opposite point of view. Its ruling was upheld by
the Court of Appeals. It was the opinion of the
court that:

"Every free man has an undoubted right to lay
what sentiments he pleases before the public; to forbid
this is to destroy the freedom of the press. . . . But
this does not mean that the Government, through agencies established by Congress, may not refuse a renewal

of a license to one who has abused it to broadcast defamatory and untrue matter. In that case there is not a denial of the freedom of speech but merely the application of the regulatory power of Congress in a field within the scope of its legislative authority."

Apparently, there are two possible definitions of censorship, and one applies to the radio and the other to the press. In the famous case of Near v. Minnesota in which the validity of the "gag laws" was tested, the United States Supreme Court held that to permit the public authorities to bring the owner of a newspaper before a judge on charges that he printed scandalous or defamatory matter and to force him "to satisfy the judge that the charges are true and are published with good motives and for justifiable ends or failing in that, to have his newspaper suppressed, is of the essence of censorship." This is the very same procedure which the Radio Commission has followed almost from the first.

But the Commission exercises an even more positive form of censorship. It is authorized under its act to "make such regulations not inconsistent with law as it may deem necessary to prevent interference between stations and to carry out the provisions of this act." Under this blanket authority, the Commission issued its Rule 177.

Writing in the *Air Law Review*,[3] Seymour N. Siegal points out:

"Congress is manifestly not permitted to abdicate or transfer to others the essential legislative functions with which it is vested. Congress may delegate its mechanical powers and certain of its discretionary powers provided there is 'a standard reasonably clear whereby the discretion must be governed.' The general rule otherwise stated is that such delegation is permissible where the policy is declared and the administrative discretion does not go to the extent of formulating the law. . . . This type of unlawful delegation was enjoined in the NRA when Congress delegated its power to make an act a crime and the Supreme Court held the delegation to the president unconstitutional."

The authority of the radio commissioners to legislate as well as to interpret and administer has not been brought to a court test. The broadcasting industry is always satisfied to leave well enough alone, and perhaps the reason why our defenders of the Constitution have been slow to attack the legislative powers of the Commission

[3] January, 1936.

is because, with the exception of the proposed rule on the rebroadcasting of foreign programs, and the statement on broadcasting by companies defying the NRA, it has thus far never been used in such a way that it has had real political or social significance. That it provides the Commission with an instrument which might be employed to end free discussion, has evoked remarkably little attention.

The Commission's ruling on lotteries shows that it has not been hesitant to do under its rule-making power exactly what it is prohibited from doing under the censorship clause of its act. Never has there been a clearer violation of the spirit, as well as the letter, of a congressional statute by a government body than the Federal Radio Commission's holding that it had no power to restrict lotteries and its statement, the same week, that it would regard the conducting of a lottery as an element in determining whether or not to renew a license. The entire legal basis of censorship by the government's radio authority is here revealed. On May 4, 1931, the American Newspaper Publishers' Association petitioned the Commission to promulgate an order banning the broadcasting of "lottery and gift programs." The Commission denied the petition in the following equivocal terms:

"To prohibit by regulation the advertisement of lottery by radio or attempt by regulation in such manner to restrict and limit the character of programs broadcast in advance of their rendition would in our opinion constitute an exercise of a power which is not expressly or even impliedly conferred by the Act. On the other hand, the construction which we place upon the Act and particularly Section 29 (the no censorship provision) thereof would seem to make it clear that Congress did not intend the Commission to exercise this power."

Three days later, the Commission issued the following statement:

"Upon frequent occasions there has been brought to the attention of the Commission complaints against radio stations broadcasting fortune telling, lotteries, games of chance, gift enterprises, or similar schemes offering prizes dependent in whole or in part upon lot or chance. On that subject the Commission has to say:

" 'There exists a doubt that such broadcasts are in the public interest. Complaints from a substantial number of listeners against any broadcasting station presenting such programs will result in the station's application for renewal of license being set for a hearing.' "

Although there was nothing in the radio law that made the broadcasting of lotteries illegal, the operators of radio stations understood that the Commission's "statement" had all the force of law. When the Communications Act of 1934 was written, the broadcasting of lottery schemes was prohibited.

Shortly after the repeal of the prohibition amendment, the Federal Radio Commission was shocked that the broadcasting industry was so unmindful of its obligation to keep the air pure as to sell time to the liquor dealers to advertise their wares. It is reported that the Commission took particular umbrage at a program broadcast by the Bamberger station WOR. The program, sponsored by the Mount Rose Gin Distilling Company of Trenton, featured a male trio known as "The Sizzlers." There was a tongue-in-the-cheek attempt to comply with the legal technicalities by having the announcer introduce the program with the statement that "those listening in from dry states may now tune out this station, for the next program is not intended to offer alcoholic beverages for sale or delivery in any state or community wherein the advertising, sale or use thereof is unlawful."

Neither this announcement nor the other liquor advertising on the program pleased the Commission. Soon it issued a statement that:

"Although the 18th amendment to the constitution of the United States has been repealed by the 21st and so far as the Federal Government is concerned there is no liquor prohibition, it is well known that millions of listeners throughout the United States do not use intoxicating liquors and many children of both users and non-users are part of the listening public. The Commission asks the broadcasters and advertisers to bear this in mind. The Commission will designate for hearing the renewal application of all stations unmindful of the foregoing, and they will be required to make a showing that their continued operation will serve public interest, convenience, and necessity."

Many radio stations heeded the warning; others had the temerity to fulfill the contracts which had been signed with the liquor trade. The Commission never carried out its threat, and soon the timid were following the lead of their braver brothers, for the liquor industry, especially in the first days after repeal, was a rich new field to cultivate. The major networks, and some independents which try the hardest to please, still refuse to accept liquor advertising.

The Commission's liquor ruling is interesting if only because the threats, the arguments, and the reasoning are typical of so many of the official ukases which have been issued. If radio stations fail to obey they are threatened with an adverse decision when they seek a renewal of their license. Then there are the little children who must be shielded and protected. Who has the audacity to make a charge of censorship when the Commission is merely trying to protect the little folks?

When the Communications Commission gathered up the reins, it not only continued the policy of issuing official regulations but it quickly formed the practice of dictating policy through speeches made before the general public, and in press statements. The holder of a broadcasting license who understands the importance of keeping track of the mental gyrations and of the whimsies of the government censors follows all speeches and press interviews with the closest attention.

In the spring of 1935, shortly after his appointment to the Commission, Chairman Prall spoke over the National Broadcasting Company's station WEAF. He declared that "radio has not taken the fullest advantages of its cultural and educational and public service possibilities. . . . Radio people would do well to eliminate programs that arouse the imaginations of children to the point where they cannot eat or sleep. . . . We cannot censor what is said on the air . . . what we can do is to maintain a general surveillance over the radio stations. If they are consistent violators [of the public interest] we can refuse to renew their licenses."

After this declaration, and several others of similar tenor, the two major networks "independently" decided that contracts with certain sponsors of children's programs should be terminated. As a sign of its desire to give the fullest coöperation to the Commission—and to the members of the radio audience—the Columbia Broadcasting System also engaged the services of a child psychologist and a group of public-spirited citizens to pass upon children's programs. The "horror hours," current when Chairman Prall issued his warning, were particularly bad. It was time that the broadcasting industry be reminded of its social responsibilities. But as the *Air Law Review* pointed out:

"Even though it has been contended, and possibly rightly so, that these extra legal powers have been utilized for the greatest good of the greatest number, it should be remembered that this is the same principle upon which European dictatorships have based their control of press and air."

VIII

YOU CAN'T SAY THAT!

O<small>N THE</small> evening of January 25, 1935, Morris
L. Ernst, one of our ablest defenders of
freedom of speech and press, arrived at the studio
of the Bamberger Department Store station
WOR, to take part in a broadcast debate on
"Balancing the Budget." In accordance with the
requirements of the broadcasting industry, Mr.
Ernst's argument had been submitted in advance
for the approval of the station's censors. As a
lawyer whose specialty is the law of libel, there
was apparently little danger that Mr. Ernst's
statements would involve the station in an action
for damages. But the censors of broadcasting
have other rules, in addition to the comparatively
simple ones of libel, according to which they determine what may be said on the air. Mr. Ernst
had not complied with the industry's unwritten
law. He had "named names," those of Rockefeller, Morgan and Ford. Before he was permitted

to face the microphone he was informed that all reference to the financiers would have to be omitted because "mention of these names might prove objectionable to interests backing advertising programs over the station." [1]

A year before, Dr. Harry W. Laidler, executive director of the League for Industrial Democracy, was told that he could not broadcast his speech on "Concentration of Control in American Industry" from Station WKY of Oklahoma City (advertised as the "pacesetter in radio progress"), unless the name of the American Telegraph and Telephone Company was deleted.

There are certain names which are held sacred by operators of radio stations. This list includes the advertisers, the financiers and the public-service monopolies—the telephone and the electric-light companies.

Because of the American reverence for the free-speech tradition, the censors of the broadcasting industry must be circumspect in the per-

[1] For this, and many other cases cited in this chapter I am indebted to the pamphlet, *Radio is Censored,* by Minna Kassner and Lucien Zacharoff, published by the American Civil Liberties Union.

formance of their duties. Therefore, the average station is operated with a specious showing of fairness and impartiality. A good example of this was the National Broadcasting Company's invitation to John L. Lewis to address the network's audience while its parent company, the Radio Corporation, was being picketed by members of a union affiliated with Mr. Lewis' C. I. O. Such outstanding exceptions, of course, do not disprove the general rule.

The operators of broadcasting stations, however, have been shrewd enough to create *causes célèbres* to which they can point when irate citizens make charges of bias. Haven't they permitted Norman Thomas, the Socialist, to broadcast; haven't they even given a national hookup to the Communists? Indeed, the Columbia Broadcasting System and the National Broadcasting Company vie with each other in making these gestures of impartiality. For 1935–36, CBS perhaps made the better score by its broadcasting of the Browder speech and its series on "Broadcasting and the American Public," in which the desirability of the present system of control was debated.

But the Browder broadcast only demonstrated again that there is no real freedom of speech on the air. The Yankee network, then an affiliated chain of the Columbia System reaching the New England audience, refused to broadcast the Communist's speech, explaining that this was done in the name of 100 percent Americanism. The next night, the network's owner, Mr. John Shephard, 3rd, permitted his listeners to hear Hamilton Fish reply to the speech which he had ruled off that part of the ether under his control. As the *Springfield (Mass.) Republican* succinctly commented, "Here was a real test of . . . impartiality and fairness in respecting the right of free speech on the air. The Yankee network failed to meet the test 100 percent exactly."

Censorship is an ugly word and the broadcasting industry prefers to describe the control it exercises as "editorial selection." [2] This phrase, coined by H. A. Bellows at one of the first con-

2 KSD, the *St. Louis Post Dispatch* station, boldly advertises in the 1936 yearbook issue of *Broadcasting* that "KSD the distinguished broadcasting station in St. Louis exercises an inflexible censorship over all programs offered for broadcasting. This protects KSD listeners and advertisers against association with the unworthy."

gressional hearings on the radio, has become most useful in the vocabulary of the broadcasting industry. Its spokesmen say that like the editors of newspapers, the managers of radio stations select, or reject, programs because of their public interest. This is an obvious untruth, for the manager of a radio station has not the same freedom as the independent editor to make his selection of material.

The government, as we have seen, exercises a restraining and frequently a guiding influence in the formulation of censorship policies. Besides this and its own prejudices, the industry has the ten-point code of ethics of the National Association of Broadcasters to guide it in determining what the American radio audience may hear. Rule 1 provides:

"Recognizing that the radio audience includes persons of all ages and all types of political, social and religious belief, each member station will endeavor to prevent the broadcasting of any matter which would commonly be regarded as offensive."

Exactly what this string of words means can be best understood by the interpretation of the word "offensive" by the various stations.

During the Simpson affair station WOR deleted mention of the name of *the* Mrs. Simpson from a program sponsored by the National Safety Bank. To avoid offending the sensibilities of their radio audience, the station censors ruled that Mrs. Simpson be referred to as "the King's dancing partner."

Shortly after "Deac" (short for deacon) Aylesworth assumed the presidency of the National Broadcasting System, he was informed by a spokesman for the electric utilities that remarks "inimical to the public utilities" were offensive. The speech to which the utilities took exception was made by Judge Rutherford of Jehovah's Witnesses. As President Aylesworth explained, the Judge had "accused the NBC of being a monopoly and it seemed best that I permit him to broadcast on July 24 [1927]. . . . It is just one of those things which is not apt to occur again in the near future."

More recently (March, 1936), station WNEW of New York refused to permit the Utility Consumers League to broadcast a speech attacking telephone rates and the special feature editor who had accepted the program was dismissed. The station's officials observed that it would be improper to lend their facilities for such a speech when the American Telephone and Telegraph Company was being investigated by the Federal Communications Commission.

While Herbert L. Pettey (now assistant manager of station WHN) was secretary of the FCC, a letter of complaint was addressed to that body because Station WHN of New York had cancelled a scheduled speech by George Slaff, one of the lawyers of the Utility Users Protective League of New Jersey. For some time this group had been a thorn in the side of the New Jersey Power & Light Company and largely through its efforts a major reduction in electric rates had been obtained. The fight that the League was carrying on was of definite public interest. This was the original opinion of the station manager, Mitchell Benson. But at the last moment, he refused to broadcast the speech. In his explanation he frankly stated:

"We are a small station trying to get along. We had better not antagonize some factions. I found it would be advisable for us to stay away from this subject. It is a matter of policy. This is a controversial subject. The matter was very interesting but was better to stay away from."

Station **WHN** did not have to worry that the government's radio authority would bring down its big stick because of its censorship policies. The attitude of the federal authority was clearly stated by Secretary Pettey in his reply to the complaint.

"You are advised," he wrote, "that not only does the Act prohibit the exercise of any previous restraint by this Commission over material broadcasted but Section 3 (H) of the Act also specifically provides that 'a person engaged in radio broadcasting shall not, insofar as such person is so engaged, be deemed a common carrier.' Thus the Commission is prohibited from censoring and upon the station licensee is placed no public utility obligation to accept any particular program material.

"In acting upon application for renewal of licenses this Commission may not consider matters over which the law has given no jurisdiction."

If this letter is accepted as an official statement of policy, no minority group, no critic of the present order, has any recourse from the arbitrary rulings of the air monopolists. That the

FCC does exert a positive censorship is beside the point. As a matter of policy, it may refuse to interfere.

The reactionary interests represented by the major chains obviously would classify criticism of the public utilities as "offensive" and controversial and therefore automatically under the ban. The program policy of the NBC specifically states that "controversial" subjects are not good material for commercial programs and must be avoided. The Columbia network has taken an even more positive stand on the sale of time for discussion of controversial public issues. Similar policies are followed by the independent stations and by members of the minor chains. This does not mean that the air waves are closed to all controversy. If it is the editorial judgment of the owner or operator of the station that the subject is sufficiently important, he may donate free time for its presentation. The series on "Broadcasting and the American Public," presented in 1936 by Columbia, was originally arranged by the Philco Radio Company as one of its regular Boake Carter programs. Columbia decreed that this was not the type of program that was fitting and proper for an advertiser to present, but offered to broadcast it as a "sustaining" feature. For this they won loud encomiums, and while busily applauding, many erstwhile critics lost sight of the high-handed policy of the network.

Strikes and other labor news have always been ticklish subjects for the broadcasting censors. William Green is, of course, a member of the advisory counsel of the National Broadcasting Company and is frequently invited to broadcast by the network. But other spokesmen of labor have found that the constitutional guarantee of freedom of speech is not synonymous with freedom to broadcast.

In December, 1936, employees of the Schenectady plant of the General Electric Company were to vote whether the company union, the Workers' Council, or the C. I. O. affiliate, the Radio Workers' Union, should represent them in collective bargaining. Spokesmen for the Radio Workers' Union asked permission to state their case in a broadcast from Station WGY, the Schenectady station owned by General Electric and managed by the National Broadcasting Company. The request was denied on the grounds that the controversy was only of "local interest" and therefore not suitable for a network station.

Two years before, the American Newspaper Guild had attempted to buy time from the seven radio stations in San Francisco to explain its side of the controversy with the *Oakland Tribune* on the discharge of three editorial workers. The Guild informed the stations that it intended to ask listeners to cancel their subscriptions to the *Tribune* as a protest against the discharge of the three men. Six of the stations, including KPO and KGO owned by NBC, and KFRC of the Columbia network, immediately refused to accept the program; the seventh, KJBS, a small station not affiliated with either of the major networks, agreed to give the Guild fifteen minutes, on the proviso that a spokesman for the *Tribune* would have an equal period in which to answer. This offer was subsequently withdrawn after the publisher of the *Tribune* had threatened the station with a libel suit "if one word of the Guild's story went on the air."

The Guild found Seattle stations more amenable during the summer of 1936 when the newspaper men were striking against Hearst's *Post-Intelligencer*. Both sides were sold time at premium rates. In this instance, the strikers had enough money to gain a fair hearing on the air. The Seattle broadcasts were, of course, acclaimed as proof that under the existing system freedom of speech is maintained on the air. Actually, it indicated nothing but the general antagonism to Hearst.

During the New York elevator strike in the spring of 1936, that ultra-reactionary, Walter G. Merritt, counsel of the Real Estate Board, told his side of the story from the broadcasting studios of WABC and WJZ, key stations of the Columbia Broadcasting System and the Blue Network of the National Broadcasting Company. The union reached a limited audience over the Debs Memorial Station, WEVD.

But in the entire record of censorship of labor news by radio stations there is, perhaps, no more revealing document than the inter-office communication issued on May 31, 1935, by the Crosley Radio Corporation, which operates two stations in Cincinnati, WSAI, and the 500,000-watt WLW. Crosley employees were informed:

"Our news broadcasts, as you have already been told, and which has been our practice for some time, will not include mention of any strikes. This also includes students' strikes and school walkouts."

Station WLW is heard by the radio audience in nineteen states. The presentation of unbiased news reports to such a vast audience should certainly be considered as a public trust. But the Crosley interests are identified with the manufacturing as well as with the broadcasting industries. For one manufacturer to broadcast news of a strike in a fellow manufacturer's plant would be aiding and abetting the common enemy. The employees of the Crosley stations were therefore given their orders. Their "independent" editorial selection was directed by headquarters.

At the time the "no strike news" order was posted, John L. Clark was the manager of WLW (Mr. Clark is now president of the Transamerica Broadcasting and Television Corporation, a company in which the Warner Brothers, of movie fame, are financially interested). Through its manager, Station WLW indignantly denied that any attempt had been made to suppress news. Yet when the Civil Liberties

Union offered to forward a photostatic copy of the original order, Mr. Clark did not boldly call for proof. He preferred to remain silent.

The Federal Communications Commission was drawn into the controversy when the evidence was presented to it for action. Again the FCC reiterated the rule that it is "precluded from directing a station to accept or reject any particular program—the sole responsibility is placed upon the station licensed."

Apparently Commissioner Payne believed that the matter should not have been disposed of in so perfunctory a manner and when Powell Crosley, Jr., appeared at one of the Commission's 1936 hearings, he took the opportunity to question the manufacturer on labor policies. The broadcasting industry was outraged. Commissioner Payne, said the trade press, was using muckraking tactics to gain publicity. It was the general consensus of opinion in the trade that the industry's linen should not have been publicly aired.

There are many other subjects which the broadcasting industry prefers not to have discussed. In the spring of 1936, Station WDAY of Fargo, North Dakota, one of the most powerful in the state, and a member of the National Broadcasting Company, canceled a scheduled broadcast by Waldo McNutt, national organizer of the American League Against War and Fascism. The station did, however, broadcast an attack on the League by Homer L. Chaillaux, national director of the Americanization Commission of the American Legion.

A few years before, the Westinghouse station KDKA of Pittsburgh refused to broadcast an Armistice Day speech submitted by the Rev. Herbert Beecher Hudnut of the Bellevue Presbyterian Church. According to Mr. Hudnut it was "a good pacifist speech." The program manager felt that "on such a day" no one should question whether "the sacrifice that our people have made for their country . . . was in vain."

On the anniversary of another historic occasion, the founding of the National Association for the Advancement of Colored People, the manager of a broadcasting station also undertook to protect the radio audience from stark realities. Before J. E. Spingarn, president of the Association, was permitted to broadcast by Station WJZ, he was told that no mention could be

made of "lynching," "race riot," and "segrega-
tion." Circumlocutions were the order of the day.
Instead of the simple word "riot," he was directed to say "trouble at Springfield, Illinois, in
which colored people were involved."

In addition to its class interest, the broadcasting industry has a "purity" fixation. This has not
prevented the broadcasting of intimate discussions by representatives of laxative manufacturers. It has, however, prevented mention of venereal diseases.

While the United States Surgeon General, Dr.
Thomas J. Parran, Jr., was New York Health
Commissioner, he was scheduled to speak over
Columbia's WABC on "Public Health Needs."
The speech was sponsored by the eminently re-
spectable National Advisory Council on Radio in
Education. Despite this and the official position
of the speaker, the network's censor wielded his
blue pencil. Dr. Parran was informed that the
following two paragraphs in their entirety would
have to be omitted:

"We have made no progress against syphilis, though
its end results crowd our jails, our poorhouses and
our insane asylums. Yet there are specific methods of

controlling it, better known to science than the methods of controlling tuberculosis. We need only to do what we know how to do in order to wipe out syphilis as a public health problem.

"In my philosophy, the greatest need for action is where the greatest saving of life can be made. I consider then, that our greatest needs in public health are first, the levelling up of present services so that every community may receive the benefits that have long accrued to the leaders; and second, a frontal attack by all communities against maternal mortality and deaths among new-born infants; against dental defects and faulty nutrition; against tuberculosis, where splendid gains have been made; against cancer and syphilis where we have done little or nothing."

That was in 1934, when Mr. Henry A. Bellows was a vice president of CBS. Now as an outsider he calls it "an error of judgment, and a clear case of censorship." Because of the rumpus caused by the Parran incident some of the broadcasters have dispensed with a little of their Nice Nellyism. Late in 1935, WNYC, New York's municipal station, permitted C. Edith Kirby, speaking for the National Society for the Prevention of Blindness, to mention syphilis as one of the causes of blindness. The *Journal of the American Medical*

Association considered this an event which merited special notice. "Municipal Broadcasting Station not Afraid" was the headline.

In 1937, the taboo on the words syphilis and gonorrhea was finally lifted by many of the more "progressive" stations. With Dr. Parran in Washington energetically waging a campaign to eradicate venereal diseases, and with the newspapers bravely printing in big headline type the two previously unmentionable words, radio stations also climbed on the bandwagon. The first series of educational lectures of this type was presented by WCAU of Philadelphia. Although the series was arranged with the cooperation of the Philadelphia Medical Society, each speech was carefully scanned by the station officials to make certain it would not offend the sensibilities of the audience.

It is, of course, the regular practice to require that radio speeches be submitted in advance and to forbid the interjection of extemporaneous remarks. The station representative who stands by with a copy of the submitted speech, the man in the control room, the owner of the station listening in at home, may give the order to throw the switch. Everyone is a censor and decisions which our jurists might ask time to ponder are instantly decided by persons inadequately qualified for this responsibility.

The excuse for this system is that the courts have held that a radio station is jointly liable with the speaker for the broadcasting of slanderous or defamatory remarks. For their own protection, the station officials point out, they must have absolute control of the material they broadcast. One of the "Freedom of the Air" bills sponsored by the American Civil Liberties Union, and introduced during the Seventy-fourth Congressional session, would have relieved the operator of a radio station of his obligation to censor, by freeing him from liability "because of anything said or done in the course of any broadcast on any public, social, political or economic issue." He would still be liable for "any defamatory, profane, indecent, or obscene language or action broadcast by any officer, employee, agent or representative of such licensee," but by limiting his responsibility, the owner of a radio station would be deprived of his most valid excuse for censorship. Despite the frequent protestations that the duty of censorship has been forced upon them, there is no record that anyone in the broadcasting industry has endeavored to obtain the speedy enactment of the bill.

The responsibility for transmitting programs which conform to standards of "good taste" is a heavy burden which the broadcasting industry has gladly assumed. Many of its rulings are ridiculous, but the station censors diligently continue to protect the American Home. Their interpretation of this duty is, to say the least, weird. The National Broadcasting Company, for instance, permitted Vince Barnett of Hollywood to use the word "damn" during his routine, but when he remarked, "I get paid good money and all the extras I can pick up," the broadcast was discontinued. Some performers are more favored than others and permitted certain liberties in the use of language. General Smedley D. Butler, formerly of the U. S. Marines, was permitted to say "damn" three times and "hell" twice during every ten minutes of his speech by one station, although another had refused to permit him to say "hell" once. Beatrice Lillie was forced to delete the word *Götterdämmerung* from one of her programs because the station was afraid some of the listeners would misunderstand, and for the same reason another comedian was prohibited from using the line, "It's been years since I've seen the old beach," but Fred Allen was permitted to announce that "Next Sunday the Reverend Dr. Jones will preach on 'Skiing on the Sabbath' or 'Are Our Young Women Backsliding on Their Week Ends?'" with a helpful emphasis on the word *ends*. According to the late David Freedman, who for many years prepared the Eddie Cantor programs, as well as those of other radio comedians, "the greatest liberty so far taken on the air was to say that Admiral Byrd's dog went crazy looking for the south pole."

Anthony Comstock, at least, trained himself by an arduous apprenticeship before he essayed the rôle of moral censor for the nation; a radio Comstock whose power and influence is far greater, may be any humorless whippersnapper in the control room of the station.

But everyone in the radio world has one inviolate rule; nothing must be broadcast which will offend the bankers, the utilities, the industrialists and the manufacturers—particularly those who advertise. Newspaper editors also exercise this type of censorship, but in the radio world the blue pencil is wielded with a heavier hand.

A few years ago, the U. S. Public Health Service made the following statement in a radio broadcast:

> "Meat is an active heat-producing food, as shown by the fact that natives of the far North live entirely on animal products, and therefore, the amount of meat eaten during the hot season should be less than that eaten during colder months."

The meat packers, who directly support broadcasting through advertising, and whose financiers are also in many instances the financiers of the radio stations, immediately protested against the "erroneous" advice of the government. Shortly thereafter the Department of Agriculture attempted to alleviate any harm that had been done to the meat interests by broadcasting that meat makes a perfect hot-weather meal.

The National Broadcasting Company protected advertisers even from themselves when Congress was holding its first public hearings on

a new Food and Drug bill. The Tugwell bill
was one in which every adult member of the radio
audience was, or should have been, interested.
But there was no discussion of the bill either by
the advertisers or by representatives of consumers. When the advertising agent for
Bristol-Myers (Ipana, etc.) asked the National
Broadcasting Company for permission to include
a two-minute speech on the measure in one of its
commercial programs, the chain's legal department ruled that the matter was of "such controversial nature that it is too dangerous to use."

According to President Paley of the Columbia
System, it was only one of the network's subor-
dinates who experienced similar apprehensions
when F. J. Schlink spoke on "The NRA and the
Consumer." The address was given at a meeting
of the Academy of Political and Social Sciences,
and although scheduled to be broadcast, it did
not go on the air. As a result of protests the president of the chain telegraphed that the action was
"wholly unwarranted and an unauthorized violation of Columbia's established policy," and Dr.
Schlink was invited to make his speech over the
network the following week. This put Columbia

into the good position generally enjoyed by the man who apologizes for a mistake.

But President Paley's apologies in no way provided assurance that similar mistakes would not be made again. It is inevitable, just so long as the stations are permitted and obliged to exercise the function of censor, that mistakes will be made. Only one thing is certain, that these mistakes will not be made against the interests of the bankers, the utilities, or the advertisers.

IX

HIS MASTER'S VOICE

U NLIKE many of his competitors, who have conducted their radio propaganda through the professional flag wavers, that rugged individualist, Henry Ford, has carried on alone and by the success of his program has demonstrated again the efficacy of Ford production methods.

Broadcasting had been going on for many years before Ford awoke to the great opportunity of using the radio to manufacture public opinion on a big scale. But he has more than made up for the years he wasted. Through his mouthpiece, William J. Cameron, who originally achieved publicity as the editor of the *Dearborn Independent* during its anti-Semitic campaign, Ford has been built up as the great and good friend of the "peepul," especially the working men, as the enemy of bankers and monopolists, and as an almost legendary figure who represents the best in the competitive system. In developing the Ford saga, Mr. Cameron has accomplished a feat surpassing even that of the publicity agent, Ivy Lee, who transformed the elder Rockefeller into a kindly old gentleman whose pockets are filled with shiny dimes.

The disservice to the public cannot be as easily estimated. If the net results of Preacher Cameron's Sunday evening talks were merely to create an idyllic picture of the automobile manufacturer, they would be of little real consequence. But they do much more than this. They constitute a one-man lobby on current legislation and on government policies; and they strive to mold, to the Ford pattern, the social and economic viewpoint of the radio audience.

Thus far, the vast majority of industrialists have been satisfied to "gang up" under the banners of The Crusaders, the Sentinels of the Republic, the Liberty League and kindred organizations, and spread their propaganda through spokesmen whom they do not publicly admit they are financing. But already the industrialists are following Ford. For example, while employees of Remington Rand were on the picket line, the company's vice president took time from the

"News Comes to Life" program, broadcast from Hearst's New York station WINS, to laud Remington Rand labor policies. It was a speech cut on the Ford pattern but lacking the Fordian subtlety.

The possibility that the microphone will become a vast sounding board for the industrialists' political, social, and economic propaganda is terrifying to anyone who correctly evaluates the power that this would give them to mold popular opinion. Under our present setup, there is no reason why the air waves cannot be so used. If Mr. Ford, whose independence of bankers' control is one of his proudest boasts, is able to convince the bank-controlled broadcasting industry that his little Sunday evening chats do not fall into the classification of controversial subjects, and that it is fitting and proper to sell time so that one man can broadcast his opinions, there appears to be no reason why other industrialists whose financial backers are also represented on the directorates of the radio stations should not be granted even greater privileges.

Some years ago, the old Federal Radio Commission ruled that "in the public interest" it would not license a broadcasting station which served merely as the mouthpiece of an individual. But the operator of a commercial station may apparently sell time on the air to any individual who has opinions which he wishes to impress on the public, and who has the money to pay to broadcast them.

There is not even a rumor that the Columbia Broadcasting System has been troubled by the demagogic nature of the Ford talks.[1] The program is, in fact, frequently cited as an example of the excellence of the entertainment jointly rendered by business and the commercialized radio industry. The approval of the public justifies this attitude. The praise of the music has been lavish and the enthusiasm for Mr. Cameron's Sunday night sermons inspires an average of two thousand fans to write him every day. Before the second year's series was completed, the Ford Company reported that requests for printed cop-

[1] Number 2 of Columbia's principles (Annual Report of the President for the Year 1935) states: "The Columbia Broadcasting System does not sell time to individuals or groups for discussion of controversial public issues such as, for example, taxation, legislation or regulation."

ies of the Cameron speeches had passed the five-million mark.

Even though some critics find the programs dull, the vast majority like to hear the old stand-bys go round and round, and then, of course, there are the Metropolitan opera stars and other expensive *virtuosi* whom the automobile manu-facturer engages for the public's enjoyment. Other merchants have been equally generous with the radio audience but Mr. Ford has gone fur-ther. In the introductory address of the first series, his son, Edsel, promised that "our program will not be interrupted by irritating sales talks. This we feel would not be fair to our friends who listen in nor would it harmonize with the charac-ter of this program." This was the perfect touch. To an audience wearied of hearing the superla-tive merits of the radio sponsor's product, and resentful of the imperative directions to show appreciation by forthwith becoming a customer, this promise was more than welcome. It made the audience friendly and receptive; it negated the impulse to turn the switch when the first half of the musical program was completed, and Mr.

Cameron came on the air to preach while the musicians rested.

According to Ford's lights, and in the opinion of the majority of the radio audience, the promise made in the first speech that salesmanship would not interfere with music has been rigidly kept. Certainly, there has never been any mention of price, no comparison of values, no announcements designed to make the listener impatient for Monday morning so that he might immediately purchase a Ford car. But there is a more subtle and an equally effective form of advertising than the continual harping on price, and it is this form which has regularly been employed in the Ford program. There are few of Mr. Cameron's speeches in which some favorable reference is not made to Ford, to Ford methods or to the superlative advantages enjoyed by Ford workers. These remarks are all by the by, and if the average listener notices them at all, he undoubtedly excuses them as natural puffing. The listener does not stop to think of the value of this indirect good-will advertising.

If Mr. Ford's evangelist would limit himself to encomiums for his master, his influence on public opinion would be of minor importance. But there was never any intention that Ford's mouthpiece would merely create good will for the automobile manufacturer and his products. The real purpose was clearly stated in Mr. Cameron's first talk.

"We propose," he said, "to bring to your attention during these programs certain matters of national interest and importance. There is need in this country at present for a better understanding of the various interest of our people, which after all are one and the same interest. . . . Our purpose . . . is to make a contribution to our country's economic health."

Preacher Cameron thereupon proceeded to extol the Ford business philosophy and labor policies, to damn bankers' control of industry, to condemn government interference, to praise the old-fashioned competitive system which gives every boy a chance to become president of the company, to ridicule the Reds and Pinks, and to glorify American pluck, ingenuity and industry. The spirit and temper of the radio audience can be fairly accurately estimated by the favorable reception which Mr. Cameron has met. Although the serious malady from which the competitive system is suffering has been diagnosed and described by able economists, the radio audience still applauds mightily when Ford's spokesman expounds his version of the "every man a king" legend.

His first chore was to make the public love his employer. The radio audience has learned that Henry Ford is not at all like the average big business man; he does not sit behind a big desk, and when he wants to talk with one of his fellow workers in the Ford plant, he goes out into the shop and holds his conference there. He never reads reports, because he knows the facts before the reports are written. However, the automobile manufacturer has time for those little things that count. "The only letters he takes time to write with his own hand are to little boy and girl friends who are having a birthday."

Like other radio salesmen, Mr. Cameron has made a regular practice of overdoing things, but apparently a statement that looks funny in print goes down better when made orally. In his first speech he prefaced a few remarks on the Ford Profit-Sharing Plan with "Naturally, *as Amer-*

ican workmen, we are all interested in the questions of labor, employment and strikes in this country, and we expect to discuss these." (Italics mine.)

This specious camaraderie and all the happy little pictures of Ford writing birthday letters do not dispel the ugly rumors about the Ford labor policies. Mr. Cameron has discussed the subject frequently, emphasizing Ford's bias in favor of the aged (men over forty) and infirm. On November 18, 1934, he reported that "twenty percent of our present workmen are in the physically disabled class. Some are blind, some deformed, some not very strong—there are twelve thousand of them in all. . . ." Mr. Cameron does not say what constitutes disability or deformity according to the Ford standards. Flat feet, knock knees, and bowed shoulders are all deviations from the norm. Impaired eyesight which requires the use of glasses is also a physical disability. It is hard, moreover, to imagine what work a blind man could perform in the Ford plant.

On layoffs and salaries, Mr. Cameron's figures sound equally good. For 1935, he reported that "59 percent of our men worked the full 52 weeks" and the average pay was $1,600.04, although the average wage of all shop employees was $1,-372.58. For 1936, Cameron promised, the record would be even better because the "famous Ford $6-a-day minimum wage" had been restored. "To tens of thousands of our men it means a clear 20 percent increase and the new rate adds $2,000,000 a month to the pay roll." The radio audience who applauded this generosity undoubtedly did not see a little news release of the Federated Press in which one of the workers in Ford's River Rouge plant reported that simultaneously with the increase in wages there was an increase in the speed-up, and a wholesale layoff. For example: "In foundry coreroom 540 men on each table before the increase turned out 17 cores a minute, three shifts working. With workers getting $6, men on each table have to turn out 20 a minute, an increase of 180 an hour, or 1,440 in eight hours. The midnight shift has been laid off, and two shifts are now turning out almost as much as the three shifts did before."

Mr. Cameron, of course, has never discussed the speed-up with his radio audience. Considering all the rumors that are current, he might have said something about it. But after all, his radio time is strictly limited, and he has many subjects to expound.

He has, in his quiet way, incited effectively against Wall Street and the big bankers. But so long as Mr. Cameron boosts the competitive system and inveighs against government interference, the bankers are, to put it conservatively, safe.

That Mr. Ford and the bankers are exceedingly friendly enemies was indicated when a group of banks, including the Chase National Bank of New York, the First National Bank of Chicago, and the National Shawmut Bank of Boston, invited Mr. Cameron to be the speaker on one of their words and music programs in 1937. The broadcasts, of course, are a direct imitation of the Ford hour, and featuring guest artists is a common practice among radio advertisers. But for the bankers to present the mouthpiece of the man who has always purported to be their arch enemy publicly established that they and the automobile manufacturers see eye to eye on fundamental problems.

Mr. Cameron has preached against government

meddling quite as frequently as he has against the bankers. Henry Ford, it will be remembered, disapproved of the NRA and created much agitation in Washington by his refusal to sign the automobile code. In his first talks Mr. Cameron pointed out that "the difference between politics and industry . . . is that we cannot just make a speech about it and consider the thing done." (December 2, 1934.) And: "Another great gain is that we have learned the best and the worst that Government can do in this matter, which is surprisingly little either way. In this job of restoring normal processes to the nation, every American must be his own leader, and every family a kingdom unto itself." (December 30, 1934.) After the NRA had been declared unconstitutional, Mr. Cameron threw off a little of his usual restraint and crowed: "Voices of Millennial prophets and harbingers of doom, formerly heard by multitudes, have ceased even to be echoes. A whole system of law erected by lawmakers has been pronounced to be lawless. Constructed of baseless fancies and colored with rainbow hues, a perfect welter of gorgeously incompetent plans faded and melted

at the first touch of reality. . . . Every attempt
to subjugate our citizens as vassals of the state
has failed. A vast sense of relief possesses the
whole people." (June 23, 1935.)

Workers who found that directly after the
NRA decision wages were reduced and hours
lengthened may not have felt this "vast sense of
relief," but for members of the radio audience
who were perplexed about the wisdom of the
Supreme Court ruling, Mr. Cameron's dictum
came as a welcome relief. The whole idea, they
suddenly discovered, was un-American.

The Washington officials, however, remained
unconvinced that the government had no right to
consider the economic welfare of the country part
of its responsibility. This recalcitrance has provided several subjects for "talks." When spokesmen for the government urged industry to re-
employ the 11,000,000 "whom Washington says
are unemployed," Mr. Cameron became highly
technical and pointed out that the lines of business classified by the government as industry
never employed more than 8,800,000 persons at
the peak. By this insistence on exact descriptions
of industry, the issue was of course confused.

This is a regular practice of Mr. Cameron. In his discussion on "business and recovery" he pointed out that industry pulled the country out of the nadir of the depression and that the effect of government spending has been negligible. "By the end of 1935," he said, "a little more than 5 billion dollars had been spent [by the government]. If you add the President's fund of 4.8 billion dollars, not yet expended, the government total is about 10 billions. Now compare that with the 27 billion dollars which American Business spent over and above its income to assist the work of recovery. . . . The use of the business surplus was the most gigantic effort that was made to keep the country going, and was by far the most effective." (March 1, 1936.)

Mr. Ford's economist failed to state that business dug into its surplus first to pay its bonded debt, dividends and high salaries to officers, and only last to pay labor. According to a study made by Leon Henderson of the NRA, security holders who profited most from the boom in the 1920's suffered least in the 1930's. For 1933 dividend and interest payments were 93 percent of those of 1923, wages were 65 percent.

Besides the steady stream of propaganda against government interference, Cameron has directly lobbied against the tax on surplus because surpluses are in fact a "form of national insurance." He has also pointed out that unemployment insurance is merely "a new political talking point . . . it simply taxes an employed man's job." (December 9, 1934.) By innuendo as well as by direct statement he has derided any attempt to improve the social and economic order by legislation. In no way must red-blooded Americans subjugate themselves to Washington.

He has also, by juggling facts and figures, indicated that America has no money rulers, that the control of wealth is not in the hands of the few but in the hands of the many. In his little talk on January 12, 1936, entitled "Who Owns the United States?" he depended for his proof on predepression figures. In 1929, he found that "the largest single block of wealth, 22 percent of the whole, was dwellings, the homes of the people, valued at 102 billion dollars. . . . Of the 25 million houses and lots in this country, 17 million are owned by their occupants, most of the others are the small investments of the same individuals. In cities, 70 percent of this property is free of mortgages, and banks hold only one-fifth of such mortgages as exist." Certainly the entire economic structure has changed since 1929 when the banks and the insurance companies began to foreclose mortgages. Mr. Cameron might easily have brought his facts and figures up to date by applying to the U. S. Department of Commerce, a source which he occasionally uses. In the same month that Mr. Cameron made his speech, the government issued a report on real-estate mortgages in sixty-one representative cities. In 84 percent of the cities, 40 to 70 percent of owner-occupied homes were mortgaged and there were a substantial number with a mortgage debt in excess of the value of the property. By using old figures, Mr. Cameron was also able to show that farmers were sitting pretty. Farms he found to comprise 12 percent of the total wealth, and "in 1930, the mortgaged farms were worth 21 billion dollars and the mortgages less than 7 billion dollars." According to House Document No. 9 (The Farm Debt Problem), the outstanding farm mortgage debt in 1930 was $9,241,390,000.

The bankers, against whom Mr. Cameron has so frequently ranted, are left entirely out of the discussion of the ownership or control of wealth. But even Mr. Cameron is not quite satisfied with the picture and he ended with the cheery note that "divided rightly or divided wrongly, *there is not enough wealth anyway.*"

Apparently all of Mr. Cameron's audience do not take his figures on faith. Despite his persuasive presentation enough of them write for the source of the figures to make it worthwhile for the Ford Company to prepare printed sheets giving the authorities upon which its spokesman relies.

Mr. Ford, or perhaps it is Mr. Cameron, looks into the future and sees that another depression is inevitable. A "period of economic rest" he calls it. He does not see, however, that a change in our present economic system may prevent such a catastrophe. If business will only prepare against a depression, if it will only build up surpluses, and if only the government does not tax those surpluses, the next depression will not be so bad as the last.

His thoughts on war and peace are more difficult to understand. Henry Ford, who financed the famous "Peace Ship," now permits his spokesman to declare: "The safety of the nation will always be preserved by those who rate some things of higher value than their lives. There will always be enough nobility among us to believe that ' 'tis man's perdition to be safe, when for the truth he ought to die.' " Later on in the same lecture he said: "Let those who dare presume to tell us what the unknown soldier would say to us today; let those who dare commit sacrilege against our dead by jeering them as having died as dupes." Mr. Cameron dares to presume because he and his employer see so clearly the menace of "the pacifism of internationalism," the red bugaboo to which he has referred frequently. Far better than this threat is war.

All of this is morbid, and Mr. Cameron refers to war only on Armistice Day. Like Pollyanna, he prefers to look at the sunny side, to turn every "stumbling block into a stepping stone," to believe that "the more anyone has of success the more everyone can have." Fallacious reasoning, economic ignorance, do not seem to trouble Mr. Cameron. It is doubtful whether the extent to which he has deluded his friends of the Sunday Evening Hour has given him a single sleepless night.

The effect on the public of the Ford-Cameron sermons is not so easy to trace as that of any of the other radio demagogues. He does not urge his listeners to bombard their legislators with telegrams, letters and petitions. But week after week he adroitly shapes their minds and thought habits. If his success continues unabated he may yet establish a production record the like of which has never been equaled by any automobile or other manufacturers; he may mold the people themselves into the Ford pattern.

X

SELLING AMERICA YOUNG

THE exploitation of children by the sponsors of radio programs and the broadcasting companies has aroused more indignation than has any other misuse of the air waves. The low level of the programs provided for adults, the direct and indirect censorship by advertisers, station officials and the federal authorities, have resulted in no such vociferous protests as have been heard against the "horror" hours.

It is much easier for the average adult to see the effect of the radio on his children than on himself. When little Johnnie has nightmares because his radio hero has been left hanging over an abyss by his fingernails, when he displays a shocking familiarity with gangster slang, when he insists that he must eat Blankety Blank's Yeast three times a day or that one packaged bread will give him greater strength than another, it requires no astute detective to discover that the radio is to blame. Parents cannot so easily trace the effect the radio has had in shaping their own language and opinions.

Thus the radio has become the *bête noir* of modern parents. The problems created for their grandparents by the ten-twenty-thirty thrillers and for their parents by the movies have been multiplied for them a hundredfold. For children, this has in truth become a radio world—a world in which synthetic radio uncles know where birthday presents are hidden, and where heroes and heroines talk and therefore to the child are real, not make-believe.

One of the NBC's advertising brochures recounts a "true story" to indicate the loyalty of children to their radio favorites and therefore, by implication, to the program's sponsors. Junior had been taken to the circus, than which, traditionally, there is no greater boon for a boy. But in the middle of one of the greatest and most stupendous acts, he asked his father the time. When he heard the hour, he jumped from his seat in great excitement. He wanted to go home immediately. If they hurried he would be in time to tune in on Little Orphan Annie.

After a survey of three thousand pupils of New York City elementary schools, Dr. A. L. Eisenberg of Teachers College, Columbia University, concluded that listening to the radio is the third principal activity of children; it is subordinate only to school and outdoor play. The average child between the ages of ten and thirteen, he reported, spends six or more hours a week at the loudspeaker. Other surveys indicate that the listening time is even higher.

Obviously, an important part of the modern child's education is derived from the radio. And what does he hear? Primarily "bedtime" stories sponsored by Big Business. Our educators are fully cognizant of the importance of radio, but so far they have been singularly unsuccessful in making use of it. Except for such programs as the Damrosch Appreciation Hour, broadcast by NBC, and the Schelling series supplied by Columbia, the radio has added nothing to cultural development. This is the charge which is regularly made. More serious is the power which has been placed in the hands of the advertiser to "educate" and indoctrinate the rising generation. Our radio stations which are licensed to serve the public interest are dependent on the bankers, utilities and patent medicine interests. We have seen how Mr. Aylesworth, for nine years president of the NBC, bribed the professors, while he was managing publicity for the National Electric Light Association, to disseminate his propaganda in the classroom. As head of a radio network he had more absolute control of what educators, addressing the larger radio audience, could say. Like every other director of a broadcasting station, if he did not like the teacher's remarks he could censor them or shut them off the air completely.

William Papier, for two years Modern Problems Instructor for the Ohio School of the Air, a division of the Department of Education of the State of Ohio, describes in detail how the stations censor educational programs.[1] Mr. Papier's lectures were addressed to students of high-school age and older, but the same type of censorship, it can be assumed, is also applied to teachers whose programs are designed for pupils in grade schools.

"When I first started to broadcast for the School of

[1] *The Social Frontier*, May, 1936.

the Air," wrote Mr. Papier, "I was told that all scripts had to be in the hands of WLW's Educational Director four to six weeks before the scheduled broadcast. Names, I soon learned, were not to be mentioned. In fact, books could not be recommended to my listeners . . . at least that was so in the case of one book I tried to recommend. Discussing the violence in the numerous strikes occurring at the time, I ignored my script at the microphone so far as to recommend Louis Adamic's *Dynamite.* The Director told me later that station WLW 'cut me off the air' until my recommendation was finished. . . .

"No further difficulties arose the first year until my script on 'Socialism' was offered. . . . The following quotation from Professor Jerome Davis of Yale was written in my original script as a final statement: 'No one can tell how far this process will eventually go, but it is only the ignorant who can say that government ownership is impossible.' WLW recommended that I drop my final quotation. . . ."

In the spring of 1935, when Mr. Papier was completing his second year of broadcasting, he was notified that his services could not be used for the last eight periods of the course. Instead of Mr. Papier's lectures on "Modern Problems," WLW announced a new series—"Modern Problems of Seniors."

With the steadily diminishing number of stations operated by colleges and other non-profit educational institutions (at the last count there were only twenty-five, and all of them were operating on undesirable wave lengths and with low transmitting power), education by radio is in the hands of the operators of commercial stations. Until there is some reallocation of wave lengths or some special arrangement for uncensored educational broadcasts, it is unquestionably better that broadcasting for children should be devoted to nothing but entertainment, even though this has been pretty bad.

The burden of providing radio entertainment for the little folks has been almost entirely assumed by Big Business for the very good reason that such broadcasting pays. Unlike some ungrateful adults who turn the dials when the sales spiel begins, the children stay on for the entire performance. And they believe what the high-pressure salesman tells them.

Only since the popularization of radio broadcasting has the importance of children in influencing the purchasing of the family been discovered. Now business knows that one of the most effective methods of increasing sales is to tell little Johnnie to tell mother to buy So-and-so's cereal to make him grow tall, to buy Such-and-such's syrup of figs ("Remind mother to ask for it by its full name") to keep him regular, to buy Blankety Blank's bread to make him strong. Formerly the patent medicine manufacturers and food processors addressed their sales talks directly to mothers; now they reach the mothers through the children.

According to a study issued by NBC, "the influence of children was found to be extremely high among purchases made by adults in grocery and drugstores," while a survey undertaken by H. P. Longstaff of the University of Minnesota, and reported in the trade journal *Broadcasting,* under the title "Are Programs for Children Worthwhile?" (for advertisers), concludes that "these programs have been very effective in inducing parents to buy the products; second, while the large part of the buying involved was undoubtedly done by the mothers, the fact remains that the real selling had been done to the children and any producer assuming women to be the hub of American buying would be overlooking a very important factor, the influence of children in determining mother's purchases. . . ."

Now that the effectiveness of increasing sales by using high-pressure methods on children has been established, it is not to be expected that the advertisers will relinquish this market, nor that the broadcasting companies will encourage them to do so. Children's programs go on the air near the supper hour, when mother is presumably busy preparing the family dinner and father has not yet returned from his day's labor. Without the little folks this would be hard time for the stations to sell. As it is, Big Business is delighted to buy it to tell stories to the children.

The pressure groups which have sprung up by the dozens to make the radio safe for Junior have been completely realistic in their approach to the problem. Their fight has not been against the control of radio education by the broadcasting companies nor the sponsorship of programs by business, but against the abuse of the privilege which business buys. By thus narrowing the line of attack, the reformers have gained some advantage. Chairman Prall of the FCC has sponsored their cause, and in conferences with the leaders of the radio industry, and in speeches, has indicated that the broadcasting of highly melodramatic programs as bedtime stories is objectionable. This dictum, issued unofficially at the annual convention of the National Association of Broadcasters in 1935, is frequently quoted as an example of the censorship exercised by the FCC. But the pressure groups were jubilant. Let others worry about the censorship power of the FCC. They were worried about Junior's nightmares.

The Women's National Radio Committee, at the time one of the most active of the "protect our home and children groups," claimed credit for the intercession of the FCC and for the new censorship regulations adopted by the Columbia Broadcasting System. As usual, Columbia saw its opportunity to acquire good will and by the early issuance of a statement of its new policies got the jump on its rival, the NBC. After a preliminary statement in which the sponsors were patted on the back—"Commercial sponsors of broadcasts addressed to children are devoting great effort and much money to creating programs that merit the approval both of child and parent," and "The Columbia Broadcasting System has no thought of setting itself up as an arbiter of what is proper for children to hear"— it issued the following rules and regulations:

The exalting, as modern heroes, of gangsters, criminals and racketeers will not be allowed.

Disrespect for either parental or other proper authority must not be glorified or encouraged.

Cruelty, greed, selfishness must not be presented as worthy motivations.

Programs that arouse harmful nervous reactions in the child must not be presented.

Conceit, smugness, or any unwarranted sense of superiority over others less fortunate may not be presented as laudable.

Recklessness and abandon must not be falsely identified with a healthy spirit of adventure.

Unfair exploitation of others for personal gain must not be made praiseworthy.

Dishonesty and deceit are not to be made appealing or attractive to the child.

This list is in itself a fairly complete outline of the type of programs which have been presented for children. As a result of the new policy, the Dick Tracy program, sponsored by Cali-

fornia Syrup of Figs and thoroughly disliked by
many mothers, went off the Columbia network.
But it did not go off the air. Tracy's adventures
with the dicks, dips and bulls continued over
Station WOR of the Mutual Broadcasting
System.

Columbia was less successful with its good-will
gesture to the Scarsdale Women's Club, whose
radio committee was among the first to issue
white lists and black lists of children's programs.
After several years of radio reviewing, the club
undertook to produce a radio script entitled
Westchester Cowboys "in an effort to determine
whether programs that satisfy parents can still
satisfy children, and also whether there is a wide
difference in taste in diverse communities." Amateur actors instead of the station's professionals
were used, not because, as was generally reported, the club was in a mood to "stick its neck
out," but because it believed that the professionals
available would not be satisfactory for the parts.
According to professional standards, the program was not a success. The women in charge
of the program claimed that the time allowed for
rehearsal was inadequate and that lack of interest

was displayed by some of the station officials. Little did it avail the ladies to protest that they were not attempting to compete with the professionals, that they merely wished to show what could be done. Unfriendly critics seized the opportunity to ridicule the reformers. *The Herald Tribune* went so far as to print a boastful interview with Mrs. George Ernst, chairman of the radio committee, who asserts that she was never interviewed by a reporter for that paper. But although the committee's efforts were ridiculed, they were by no means unsuccessful. A majority of the twenty-two hundred children who listened in liked the program and asked for more "about the same Peter, please." Wilderness Road, a program arranged and sponsored by Columbia, and rated as one of the best for children in the 1935–36 season, was directly inspired by the Westchester Cowboys.

The sensitiveness of CBS to the opinions of lady reformers was indicated again in 1936 when there were wholesale "resignations" by executives in the program department after the Women's National Radio Committee announced their list of approved children's programs. Of the twelve approved programs,[2] only three were broadcast by CBS.

It is significant that of the twelve programs, eight were sustaining features produced by the stations without advertising sponsorship. Apparently, a program that does not have to sell goods can more easily meet the standards of parents and teachers. But the mother who undertakes to censor the radio entertainment of her children and who goes to the trouble of learning at what time, and on what stations, sustaining programs are being broadcast is defeated in the end. For the program which the child has learned to follow may suddenly turn commercial. As the NBC points out:

"While the children's program department of the National Broadcasting Company has pointed the way to good taste in children's programs, we must admit that sponsored children's programs hold the greatest

[2] American School of the Air, CBS; Animal Closeups, WJZ—Blue Network; Animal News Club, WJZ—Blue Network; Billy and Betty, WEAF—Red Network; Captain Tim Healy, WJZ—Blue Network; Damrosch Appreciation Hour, Red and Blue Networks; Junior Radio Journal, WJZ—Blue Network; Singing Lady, WJZ—Blue Network; Spare Ribs, WEAF—Red Network; Standard School Broadcast, NBC; Story Teller's House, WOR—Mutual; Tom Broadhurst's Sea Stories, CBS; Wilderness Road, CBS (only programs on the national networks were considered).

juvenile attention and that the best the National Broadcasting Company has had to offer in this field have been
quickly appropriated by sponsors who desire to hold
the interest of children not only in the entertainment
program but in the products sold by the sponsor to a
friendly juvenile audience."

Stated a little more baldly, the broadcasting
companies produce sustaining programs only in
the hopes of selling them to sponsors. Since their
business is carried on for profit, they cannot afford the luxury of regularly providing programs
merely because they are good for children.

Frequently parents and children disagree
about which programs are good and which are
bad. The approved children's programs reported
by Parent-Teachers' Clubs are frequently at va-
riance with the choice of the children themselves.
This makes an excellent argument for the sponsors who wish to prove that after all they know
more than the mother about what children like.
But business men are now learning that it isn't
smart to antagonize mother.

An analysis of the approved lists of the various
pressure groups shows that there is a decided preference for the programs of sponsors whose prod-

ucts the parents approve. The Singing Lady of the Kellogg Company ("Ask mother to get you a package of Rice Krispies—the singing cereal") is regularly offered as an example of a completely satisfactory program. In addition to singing the praises of the cereal, the Singing Lady presents a program of nursery rhymes.

Like the product, the program is pleasant and harmless. Mothers may know that for the nourishment derived from the singing cereal its cost is high. But Rice Krispies may induce children to drink more milk, and the processed food is therefore considered desirable by families whose budgets permit. The excessive cost of Jell-O has been publicized by consumer groups. But many children like gelatine desserts, and for the average child they cause no digestive disturbances. Mothers therefore are satisfied not only with Jell-O's radio show but also with the persistence of its radio salesman, for at the end of the performance the children may go into the kitchen and make a batch of Jell-O. But when the sponsor's product is not one that the parent approves, or when in his attempt to build sales the advertiser shows little regard for the health or well-being of his audience, then the parents object loudly. When the manufacturers of Tastyeast urged their little friends of the radio audience to munch the chocolate-covered yeast three times a day, the parents definitely protested.

This is only one instance when the advertiser overplayed his hand. In the past, the sponsors of children's programs regularly resorted to threats and blackmail to increase sales. Children have been told that the hero would die, or that the story would be discontinued (always at a point of high excitement) unless the advertised product was immediately bought. A more ingenious appeal was used by Wheaties. The children were told that one of the characters named in the broadcast required medical attention and that proceeds from the sale of the processed cereal would be used to defray these charges. When General Mills, Inc., manufacturers of Wheaties, stipulated with the Federal Trade Commission in July, 1936, that such announcements would be discontinued, it also agreed to cease advertising that the whole wheat from which Wheaties is made contains almost twice the body-building protein of corn.

Although outright blackmailing is now considered in poor taste, the gullibility of children is still regularly played upon. When little Johnnie is told by the friendly radio voice that a certain processed cereal, canned milk, packaged bread or laxative will make him grow strong, or that it will help him to be the star of the team, he believes it. The debunkers of advertising who have made a not inconsiderable portion of the adult audience skeptical of the superlative claims advanced for processed foods and patent medicines, should now write a primer for children. Subjected as they are to the wheedling of the radio artists, they need some lessons in building a defense. A youngster who is not old enough to discriminate, who believes everything he is told, and who has been taught to accept the words of his elders as truth, is the readiest of all game for the advertiser. He starts to be a sucker when he is just getting into knee breeches.

In the *Psychology of Radio*,[3] the authors recount an incident from the life of a seven-year-

[3] By Hadley Cantril and Gordon W. Allport. Published by Harper & Bros., New York, 1935.

old radio fan who was directed to "do a favor" for the heroine of the broadcast story by telling his mother about the advertised product, a chocolate flavoring for milk. The mother was one of those cynics who is unimpressed by advertisers' ballyhoo. She therefore turned to her consumer's guide and learned that the product "has no significant advantage over cocoa prepared with milk in the home . . . and as such mixtures are generally unwarrantedly expensive, none is recommended." But this report did not save the family's purse, for Andrew insisted that his radio friend had told him the chocolate milk would give him added "pep" and mother's arguments were less convincing than those of the radio salesman. Andrew got the chocolate beverage.

The "pep" appeal is one of the most popular with the radio sponsors. Generally it is used in combination with the appeal to the "joining instinct" of children. There are few radio sponsors who have not established clubs, teams, or secret societies which their fans can join, not because they excel in anything, but merely because they can collect a dozen box tops, or half a dozen wrappers, each one, of course, representing a sale of the product. By means of the box tops, the sponsor can gauge the interest of the children in his program. When the bundles of box tops or wrappers decrease in size, the program must be changed or snapped up. Of course the children do not understand the reasons for the clubs, but their mothers may. If they are indulgent, and can afford the expense of purchasing the necessary number of articles, Junior sends in his box tops and gets his badge. If, for any reason, mother decides that she knows best, and that Junior should not become a member of the club, there is the devil to pay. Junior nags, mother scolds, and in the end one must give in. Usually it is mother. Junior believes what the radio voice tells him far more readily than he does what mother has to say.

Since the blackmail threats have been discountenanced, the premium appeal has been played heavily, until it has become not only a private but also a public nuisance. In the March, 1936, issue of the *Radio Review,* it was reported:

"Ralston's would be delighted, no doubt, to know that in the Borough of Queens, New York City, a few weeks ago, boys were canvassing from house to house for package tops. The idea, it seems, was for several

to pool their spoils to see if the result of this united
effort would not win a hundred dollar check for 'the
gang.' . . . "

The newer type of advertising on children's
programs is being aimed almost directly at
mother. Swift & Co. was one of the leaders in
sponsoring children's programs for a product in
which a child can have absolutely no interest. In
the publicity releases announcing the "Junior
Nurse" broadcasts, which advertise Sunbrite
cleaner, parents were promised that every program would be passed upon by a psychiatrist and
that

"While the broadcasts will take full advantage of the
love of adventure and the hero-worship that is inherent
in every child, parents will not have to worry about
letting their children listen to these programs. There
has been so much talk about the possible ill effects of
certain children's programs that we believe mothers will
appreciate our efforts to give their children entertainment that is certified pure, and that this appreciation
will be expressed in increased purchases of Sunbrite."

To become a member of the Junior Nurses, the
applicant must send in labels from cans of
Sunbrite. In a three-month period, between

February and April of 1936, seven thousand children had joined. This record, even though encouraging, is not so good as that made by the Scoop Ward Press Club, which reported that in seven weeks' time its membership had reached two hundred thousand. Possibly the certificate of purity was not so effective after all.

The success of the Uncle Don broadcasts, now in their eighth year, is perhaps the most vivid example of the mediocre standards approved by some mothers. This synthetic uncle, who "will mention your product or service before and after each daily program and give it a complete half hour once each week for $700," [4] has had one of the most amazing successes of any radio entertainer. His programs are heavily ladened with advertising announcements. But Uncle Don names names (sent him by parents) of boys and girls who suck their thumbs, who refuse to study, who run across the street, or who are otherwise nuisances. The effect on a child of hearing his name broadcast is almost miraculous. That the public censure by Uncle Don is an open admission by mother of her lack of control does not

4 Advertisement in *Variety*, March 25, 1936.

bother the good ladies who write to the sympathetic and synthetic uncle. It is these ladies who are bewildered when they hear some of their more cynical sisters decry the effect of commercialized broadcasting on the rising generation.

XI

TAKING IT TO THE PEOPLE

THE 1936 presidential election proved the power of the radio as has no other single event in the history of the country. Any question of the comparative strength of the press and the radio was conclusively settled by the electorate when it returned President Roosevelt to office with a landslide vote. The press opposed reëlection; the President spoke to his friends of the radio audience.

The broadcasting stations took no sides—they are prohibited from doing so by law. The legal requirements were, of course, not mentioned in the praise of the broadcasting industry for its impartiality.

The Democratic party had a single but most important advantage over the Republicans in the radio campaign. President Roosevelt is unexcelled as a radio performer; Alfred E. Landon gave bad performances.

Showmanship has become a prime essential of the candidate for political office—showmanship of a different order than that required by former presidents who could win an election by talking to "the folks" from his back porch.

Broadcasting has effected other and more significant changes in campaign technique. Long before the heat and fury of the 1936 campaign, Owen D. Young declared:

"Freedom of speech for the man whose voice can be heard a few hundred feet is one thing. Freedom of speech for the man whose voice may be heard around the world is another. . . ." [1]

Any indignation aroused by Owen D. Young's suggestion of a double standard for freedom of speech was just so much waste emotion. For since 1932 a different rule has applied to political speakers whose remarks are broadcast than to those who are content not to have their words amplified; the first are subjected to the censorship of the broadcasting companies, the second need only comply with the police regulations. This situation exists despite the apparent efforts

[1] Speech at Rollins College, Florida, February 24, 1936.

of the lawmakers to assure continuity of that most revered of American concepts, freedom of speech.

As far back as 1926–27 when the Radio Act was being drafted, the political potentialities of the new medium were already understood. This foresight on the part of the legislative draftsmen prompted the inclusion in the Act of a specific provision:

"If any licensee shall permit any person who is a legally qualified candidate for any public office to use a broadcasting station he shall afford equal opportunities to all other such candidates for that office in the use of such broadcasting station, and the Commission shall make rules and regulations to carry this provision into effect:—Provided, that such licensee shall have no power of censorship over the material broadcast under the provisions of this section."

The lawmakers were taking no chances. When the Communications Act was written, this provision was carried over verbatim. Even though the important clause prohibiting censorship of political speeches had been nullified by the courts, the second set of draftsmen apparently felt that they could not improve on the work of their predecessors.

Like so many other much-touted safeguards, this provision has proved to be inadequate. During the 1936 campaign, there were several incidents which clearly demonstrated its weakness as well as its strength, but as almost invariably happens, the general public was much more impressed by the second than by the first.

It was no other than William Randolph Hearst who gave proponents of the American system a beautiful opportunity to show how effectively and equitably broadcasting is regulated in these United States. If they had been able to arrange the entire affair themselves, they could not have done better. Several weeks before Hearst solemnly announced that President Roosevelt was in cahoots with the Communists, the NBC Red Network, of which Hearst's Pittsburgh station WCAE is a member, broadcast a speech by Earl Browder, Communist candidate for the presidency. WCAE refused to take the program. As a result of the protests immediately filed with the station and the Federal Communications Commission, Emil J. Gough, vice president of Hearst Radio, explained that the speech had not been broadcast because "it had another program for that hour which it regarded as of greater public interest." This program was an advertisement for the *American Weekly,* the sensational Sunday supplement of Hearst newspapers. Equally important programs might have popped up on the dates of the other three Communist speeches called for in the NBC contract if the Communications Commission had not informed WCAE that the section on political broadcasting applied to Communists as well as to Republicans, and to Hearst stations as well as to all others. The penalty for violation of the section, according to Order No. 178, may be revocation of the broadcasting license. Only after this penalty had been called to the attention of the Hearst officials did they agree to broadcast the remarks of the Communists. The *New York Times* quoted Mr. Gough as saying:

"But for these mandatory provisions of law and the regulation of the Commission heretofore referred to [that failure to comply might mean loss of license and heavy fines] station WCAE would reject the Browder program in full."

Thus over one of his own stations Mr. Hearst was attacked as "fascist-minded" and as one of the reactionaries who "will stop at nothing to push through their sinister plans."

Here, cried defenders of the present system, is complete proof that the American way assures freedom of speech. The Hearst incident was indeed cause for jubilation. It proved conclusively that if there is sufficient public protest, the FCC will step in and prevent gross flaunting of the law. It does not, unfortunately, assure anything like freedom of speech on the air to political candidates.

Even though by law the broadcasting companies are forbidden to discriminate against particular candidates or parties, and even though censorship of political speeches is explicitly prohibited, the interpretation and application of the law make both possible.

Two years before the passage of the Communications Act, the Nebraska Supreme Court held a radio station jointly liable with a political candidate for a broadcast which the court found to be libelous.[2] According to the court's interpretation of the federal provision:

"The prohibition of censorship of material broadcast over the radio station of a licensee merely prevents the licensee from censoring the words as to their political and partisan trend but does not give a licensee any privilege to join and assist in the publication of a libel nor grant any immunity from the consequences of such action."

It is legal quibbling to say that the radio station must censor political speeches to prevent libelous remarks and still conform to the terms of the federal provision by not censoring the political import of the speech. In the average political address, one is usually too closely bound to the other to permit of separate treatment.

The test case presented an interesting set of circumstances. In 1930 Senator Norris was campaigning for reëlection and Station KFAB had permitted him to broadcast. An invitation was then extended by the station to Senator Norris' opponent, W. M. Stebbins. The latter decided

2 Sorenson v. Wood and KFAB Broadcasting Company; 243NW82.

not to speak for himself but, like Miles Standish
in the Longfellow epic, to let a friend plead his
cause. His spokesman was Richard F. Wood,
candidate for state railway commissioner. Apparently Wood decided to avail himself of the opportunity to speak for himself as well as for his
friend, and it was some of these remarks that resulted in the action for libel. In discussing the
record of C. A. Sorenson, a candidate for re-
election as state attorney general, Mr. Wood
said:

"In his [Sorenson's] acceptance of the attorney general's office he took an oath before God and man that he
would uphold the law justly and honestly. His promises to man are for naught, and his oath to God is
sacrilege, for he is a non-believer, an irreligious liber-
tine, a mad man and a fool."

A little later along he pointed up this description by promising that:

"If you see fit to reward me for my efforts for clean
government, I will serve you and every section of this
state fearlessly as I have in dealing with the Judas
Iscariots of our state and party."

Considering the scurrilous attacks which have

been made with impunity by our demagogues (Judas Iscariot was always a popular description with Father Coughlin) and by political speakers, the Wood remarks do not seem to justify special action. In the course of his harangue, however, Wood also charged that Sorenson had favored the gambling racketeers. Sorenson disproved this, and a jury in the district court awarded him damages in the amount of $1 for the injury to his reputation. The radio station was not held jointly liable by the trial court, but this portion of the decision was reversed by the state supreme court. This holding, that radio stations are legally answerable for libelous remarks which they permit candidates for political office to broadcast, has never been overruled.

The effect of the decision was concisely stated by the Committee on Communications of the American Bar Association. It observed that:

"Speeches by or in behalf of opposing candidates for political office frequently contain matter which, if untrue, may be actionable defamation. Only by permitting such utterances may the misdeeds of office holders and of candidates be exposed to the public.

"Freedom of speech by radio in the sense and to the

degree seemingly implied by Section 18 of the Radio
Act (Section 315 in the Communications Act) becomes
a delusion as a practical matter if the privilege is given
to, or the responsibility is placed on, the broadcaster
to censor a political speech for alleged defamatory
utterances." [3]

But the obligation to censor political speeches
is placed on the broadcasting companies, and although their managers or owners may have no
training in the intricacies of the law, nor their
legal advisers be gifted with the wisdom attrib-
uted to the nine old men of the United States
Supreme Court, they must decide whether certain charges are true and can be proven, or even
when true, whether it is advisable to permit them
to be broadcast. In order to determine whether
a speech is safe, the program director may demand a copy of it in advance, and fortified with
the excuse that he must protect himself and his
station against actions for libel, blue pencil any
remark which displeases him. It is obvious that
to permit the broadcasting company this privilege completely vitiates the effectiveness of that
part of the law which guarantees to all political

[3] American Bar Association Report, 1932, page 24.

candidates equal opportunity to be heard on the
air. To allow a candidate to broadcast is an
empty privilege if the broadcasting company
may dictate what he may and may not say.

It is also obvious that the station censors will
scrutinize most carefully the speeches of candidates of the minority parties. It is the Communists, the Socialists, the EPIC spokesmen who
may say dangerous things.

During the 1936 campaign, WTCN of Minneapolis, owned by the Minnesota Broadcasting
Corporation, had signed a contract for a series
of campaign broadcasts by spokesmen of the
Communist party. Nat Ross, candidate for presidential elector, was to be the first speaker, and
well in advance of the broadcast the speech was
submitted to the station for approval. The station censors did not like it, and demanded the
elimination of a number of paragraphs. The
Communist party decided to withdraw the speech
entirely and to try again. This time it submitted
a speech to be made by Sam K. Davis, who was
not a candidate for any office. The speech was
approved. Just before beginning his broadcast
Davis asked permission of the announcer to make

a slight addition. His request was granted, and he went on the air. But no sooner had he finished than the station cancelled the rest of the series. By making the change, it said, the contract had been violated. After protests by the Civil Liberties Union and threats of mandamus proceedings, the station agreed to continue broadcasting the series.

When Upton Sinclair was campaigning for the governorship of California, he was subjected to the same kind of badgering by the broadcasting companies.

"One trying feature was that I was forced to submit copy in advance; and having to read a speech takes all the life out of it for me. But the big stations asserted that Federal regulations required this. I noticed when I went East after the primaries, that Federal regulations did not apply. In Chicago, Washington and New York I was invited six or eight times to say whatever I pleased. I noticed that on election night the barriers went down even in California, and both Columbia and NBC chains gave me time and told me to 'shoot the works!' " [4]

Mr. Sinclair undoubtedly should have known

[4] Letter to the author, dated March 11, 1936.

that the federal regulations explicitly prohibit censorship. But even had he known this, and pointed it out to the broadcasting companies, he still would have been subjected to the same restrictions.

In their dealings with the radio stations, the minority parties also have a financial handicap. The law requires that all candidates are to be afforded equal opportunity to broadcast. But this privilege must be paid for. The Democrats and the Republicans, of course, have big war chests on which to draw, but the minority parties are poor. At present, the financial handicap of the minority parties is increased by the practice of extending credit to the major parties while requiring the minor parties to pay in advance. It was not until February of 1936 that the Democratic National Committee settled with the two major networks for its radio campaign in 1932. The Republicans had cleared the books a few months before.

Compared to the radio bills for 1936, the ones for 1932 were picayune. Approximately $500,-000 was spent during the Roosevelt-Hoover campaign; in 1936 Democrats, Republicans and

minor parties used more than $2,000,000 of time
on the air. The major networks, which received
the lion's share of the campaign funds, made
a state secret of their billings and refused to di-
vulge the amount charged the various parties.
The Republican *New York Herald Tribune,*
however, estimated that the Republican National
Committee's radio bill was $800,000 and that of
the Democrats, $500,000. State and local com-
mittees added many more thousands to the expenditures for radio of the major parties. The
Communist party invested more than $65,000 in
broadcasting; the Socialists were more economi-
cal, spending approximately $30,000. The
Townsendites, the Union Party, the Jeffersonian
Democrats, the Independent Coalition of American Women, and the other special groups spent
an estimated $300,000. The cost of taking it to
the people was high.

During the campaign period, it is chiefly the
minority parties which protest against censorship. But before the 1936 campaign started, the
Republicans were also entering protests. They
had attempted to get the jump on all rivals by

buying time from the national networks for the presentation of a series of dramatic sketches lampooning the New Dealers. "Liberty at the Crossroads" was the title, but the Republicans soon discovered who controls the liberty to broadcast. Both major networks turned thumbs down on the program, and although the NBC attempted to placate the Republicans by promising them broadcasting privileges from "time to time," the Columbia network issued a clear-cut statement of the standards according to which it censors political programs.

First of all, an open and closed season was declared for political broadcasting. The open season starts after the regular national party conventions, which are broadcast by both networks free of charge,[5] and ends on election day. During this period, when the provisions of Section 315 apply, Columbia (and the NBC)[6] is willing to sell time to political parties. In the closed season,

[5] NBC's statistical department estimated that it cost the network $265,000 to broadcast the Republican and Democratic conventions. This figure includes the value of the commercial contracts which were canceled.

[6] The NBC has not publicly subscribed to these policies, but in practice they have followed them, and the dicta of the CBS can therefore be accepted as that of both major networks.

it will donate time to political speakers whose messages, in its editorial judgment, is of public interest. Thus the network officials have become the supreme arbiters of political discussion. Answering the charge made by the Honorable Henry P. Fletcher, chairman of the Republican National Committee, that this constitutes absolute censorship, President Paley wrote that this policy "is based upon our belief that we are charged with a public duty to allot time for free discussion of controversial public questions including politics, and we refuse to sell time for this purpose." This high-minded policy bows to commercial exigencies during the campaign periods.

In addition to the ruling on the closed season, President Paley also stated that at no time would dramatization of political issues be permitted. Quoting from a letter which had been written earlier in the controversy, he explained that:

"Appeals to the electorate should be intellectual and not based on emotion, passion or prejudice. We recognize that even the oratorical discussions of campaign issues can be to a degree stamped with the aforementioned flaws but we are convinced that dramatization would through the radio campaign almost wholly overdo the emotional side. . . ."

No one before had ever presumed to dictate what kind of show the Republican Party should put on. Now the broadcasting companies were not only attempting but were successfully dictating in what form political harangues must be arranged, and when politics might be discussed. It was enough to make even a Republican see red.

In the end, however, the joke was on Columbia. WGN, the *Chicago Tribune* station, found the Liberty skits acceptable, and after the first broadcast the press printed the dialogue in part or in whole. Heywood Broun, in a dramatic criticism, reported that "Mr. Fletcher's first campaign show is a sort of Republican 'shoot the works' and that is putting it mildly. The Democrats who have been having a tough time lately can afford to laugh at last. Their attitude toward their adversaries ought to be 'just give them enough radio.' " The whole story became news and the March of Time thereupon broadcast most of one sketch during its regular program over the Columbia network. Apparently the station censors did not feel that the sketch would be as dangerous to the electorate when presented by *Time*; or perhaps they were glad to have the whole thing finished and over with, without bearing the real responsibility for the broadcast.

But Chairman Fletcher was   not satisfied. When the major chains arranged a national "hookup" for President Roosevelt's address to Congress on January 3, 1936, and again five days later when the President made the principal address at the Jackson Day dinner, the Republican chairman pointed out that both speeches were partisan and political, and that his party should be granted equal privileges. Wrote President Paley: "I am glad to answer your question as to whether or not the time we allotted for the President's speech was a donation to a political party. It certainly was not. It was a donation to the American people. It has always been our policy to make time available for the President of the United States when he wishes to address the nation. We followed this policy through two Republican administrations and we follow it now."

The broadcasting companies know that failure to make such donations of time to the First Citizen may have unpleasant results. Station KFI of Los Angeles failed to broadcast one of the Fireside Chats. During the campaign period, the Democratic National Committee bought the entire NBC Red Network for President Roosevelt's Syracuse address, but pointedly omitted KFI. To reach the Los Angeles territory, the Columbia station KHJ was signed up. Shortly before the broadcast, the NBC network officials persuaded the National Committee to broadcast the speech through KFI as well. In the midst of the controversy it was reported that the Communications Commission had authorized station WGAN of Portland, Maine, to proceed with the construction of a new transmitter and operate on KFI's clear channel.

The handling of political programs is a particularly trying task for the broadcasting companies. They wish to offend no one, yet they may offend everyone. Certainly they do not wish to antagonize either of the major parties, for either one may win, and on the administration in office depends the favors extended to the radio station.

After the last election, H. L. Pettey, who managed the Democratic Radio Campaign, became secretary of the FCC. Who can prophesy which one of the radio managers of the major party may be the next secretary, or even a commissioner? Candidates of the minor parties have no such potential power, but even they must be treated with a show of fairness.

The broadcasting companies would have a far easier time if they had not presumed to act as the Emily Posts of the air and to rule on the niceties of political conduct.

In the closing days of the 1936 presidential campaign, the publicity directors of the Republican party conceived a "stunt" program which, journalistically at least, was the brightest of the entire campaign. Phonograph records of speeches made by President Roosevelt when he was a candidate in 1932, and of other of his early addresses, were culled for remarks and promises of which the Republicans felt that the President— and the electorate—should be reminded. These statements were then reproduced on another record. The idea was to use the President's recorded voice in a broadcast "debate." Senator

Arthur H. Vandenberg was selected to present the Republican argument, and he appeared at the broadcasting studio in person. When Mr. Paley and his associates learned what the Republicans were planning they were thrown into a complete dither. The entire broadcast was without precedent. Should they permit the President's recorded voice to be broadcast; should they not? Until the moment that the program went on the air they were undecided. This indecision further complicated the situation because the entire program was broadcast by some members of the Columbia network, while by orders from New York headquarters it was shut off others a few minutes after the broadcast began. The official explanation was that the program violated the company's policy against the broadcasting of electrical transcriptions, a rule originally established to protect artists and composers against infringement of their rights.

For the Republicans, the stunt was well worthwhile. The press gave the "debate" wide publicity. No other campaign speech of either party attracted as much attention. The propriety of the broadcast and the Columbia policy was ques-

tioned.[7] Is a broadcasting company to determine rules of etiquette for campaign speakers?
Until the days of broadcasting the electorate indicated on election day which party had erred in
the presentation of its case. The broadcasting
companies have now presumed to come between
the electorate and the political campaigners.

It is frequently rumored that if they could, the
broadcasters would keep clear of the entire polit-

[7] The method of presentation made it clear that the President
was not present in person. Senator Vandenberg was introduced
thus:

"Tonight, ladies and gentlemen, Senator Arthur H. Vandenberg, of Michigan, an outstanding Republican leader and
member of the United States Senate, is here to conduct a
'fireside chat.' It is agreed by all that when a man seeks public
office and makes public statements to influence public opinion
his words become public property. Newspapers, magazines,
authors and public speakers have the unquestioned right to
quote such statements without limit. It is only thus that we
are able most faithfully to compare the words of a man with
his deeds. Without further delay, therefore, I shall turn the
microphone over to Senator Vandenberg to open this new kind
of fireside chat."

A minute later the announcer again explained:

"Ladies and gentlemen, this is Mr. Pratt speaking again.
Mr. Roosevelt, the candidate, is here in voice but not in person.
Through the miracle of science his voice has been preserved.
Therefore, whenever you hear him talk again during this broadcast it will be his own actual voice, taken from the air in 1932
and 1933 at the time his statements were made and brought to
you tonight in this most unusual radio program. I now turn
the microphone back to you, Senator Vandenberg."

ical broadcasting business. It is true that during campaign periods the major parties are among the biggest buyers of time (out of season the free time they demand costs the stations many a pretty penny) and even though they do not pay their bills promptly, eventually the broadcasting companies do collect. Yet, despite the revenue from political broadcasting, the trouble it causes and the problems it creates are enough to make the broadcasting companies desirous of keeping their fingers out of the sticky political pie.

Many plans have been suggested to relieve the broadcasting companies of their present political responsibilities. The adoption of the Wisconsin plan for national use is frequently offered as a possibility. In Wisconsin, WHA, a state-owned and -controlled station, sets aside a definite hour every weekday for state legislators to broadcast to their constituents on current legislative affairs. No legislator or state official has ever been refused time on the air, and no one has suggested improper use of the facilities. During campaign periods time is also given free to all candidates, including those representing minority parties.

In the legislation originally introduced by Representative Byron Scott of California in August, 1935, there was a proposal to utilize the present commercial setup but to rewrite Section 315 to provide that each radio station "shall be required to set aside (without charge) regular and definite periods at desirable times of the day and evening for uncensored discussion on a nonprofit basis of public, social, political, and economic problems. . . ." The station was to have no liability for material so broadcast, and something nearer free political speech would have been achieved. Thus far, Congress has not seen fit to act on the proposal.

During the Columbia sponsored debate on "Broadcasting and the American Public," Norman Thomas answered the hypothetical question, "Do you think time for political discussions revolving around controversial issues should be sold just like other time on the air?" with the suggestion that as part of the price of their use of the wave length the stations be required to give an agreed amount of time for political discussion, to be shared by the various political parties. Extra time which the stations decided to allot to political subjects might then be bought on the regular commercial terms.

William Hard suggested in his speech at the Sixth Annual Institute for Education by Radio (1935) not only that the broadcasting companies donate free time for all political parties during a national presidential campaign, but that this time should be divided with an eye to favoring the financially weaker parties. This was another suggestion for which the broadcasting companies evinced no enthusiasm. For, as David Lawrence pointed out, "since when has it become the business of radio companies to attempt to correct economic or social inequalities?"

XII

AIRING THE NEWS

WHEN the American Newspaper Publishers
Association met for its annual conclave in
1936, the press-radio war was almost over—ending like a Chinese fiasco with enemy openly
trading with enemy.

Only the diehards still refused to make terms.
Edward H. Harris, chairman of the Association's radio committee, made the meeting hall
resound with his protest:

> "The sale of news to any broadcasting station or to
> any advertiser for sponsorship over the air is just as
> unsound as if the newspapers sold news to their adver-
> tisers and then permitted them to commingle this news in
> their advertising copy. How long would the newspapers
> hold the confidence of the public as media for the dis-
> semination of information if they adopted such a
> policy?"

But these stirring words could not renew the
fighting spirit of the publishers. Their crusade

against radio's "prostitution" of the news had been basically an economic struggle. The press-radio war began when the publishers discovered that the broadcasting industry was making serious incursions into their circulation and advertising income. Peace was unofficially declared, when the leaders of the press recognized that their best financial course lay not in fighting a competitor, armed with a weapon more potent than theirs, but in joining forces with it.

The social consequences of this "state of peace" are far-reaching. The publishers may no longer be outraged by the direct control of Big Business over the broadcasting of news. But this does not mean that the danger implicit in such control has been eliminated.

It is no secret that advertisers exert an indirect influence over newspaper columns. But never, until the advent of popular broadcasting, was news interpreted for the public by men who received their weekly pay checks directly from the business rulers of America.[1] And never before

[1] According to a survey reported in *Variety* (October 7, 1936), "oil companies topped the list of newscast bankrollers and the most consistent local buyers of that product were department stores. . . . Among the petrol refiners the big underwriters of

has a single reporter told his story to so large and widespread an audience.

The business reasons which motivated the newspaper publishers in their battle against the sponsorship of news broadcasts by advertisers are transparent, if only because of their attitude toward the news commentators. Throughout the press-radio war, the right of the refiners, manufacturers and bankers to present interpretations of the news went practically unchallenged. What the publishers decried was the broadcasting of "spot" news and the reason why is obvious. Members of the radio audience who tune in on the news bulletins can get the news without buying a newspaper; those who listen only to the commentators must still read the papers. It is entirely true that by the omission of certain items from the news bulletins, or by the form of presentation, the radio audience may be misinformed or prejudiced. For example, in one of the first Esso news programs broadcast by a national broadcasting company, the crash of the United Air liner in Wyoming, the big news story of the

---

news broadcasts were the various (Rockefeller) Standard Oil entities and the Tide Water Company."

day, was entirely omitted. But the failure to include news of the disaster was not as notable as the explanation made by Frank Mason, NBC vice president, that the "chain does not feel that it has a responsibility to its listeners to supply all the news and that 'radio is an entertainment and educational medium.' " [2]

The opportunities of the commentator to color news is infinitely greater than that of the news reporter. His status in the radio world is similar to that of the editorial writer—he not only reports but he also interprets. That it is actually and potentially more dangerous for these men to be the hirelings of Big Business, the publishers apparently ignored. Even when the publishers asserted their right to protect the freedom of the press, and dictated the terms governing the broadcasting of news, the only suggested limitations on the commentators' performances were that they be generalizations, and that spot news be eliminated.

The average news broadcaster, like the average newspaper man, publicly denies that the advertiser dictates or influences what may be said, but

[2] *Editor and Publisher,* October 12, 1935.

the gagging of Alexander Woollcott by his Cream of Wheat sponsors, and the proudly advertised boast of Philco that Boake Carter expresses "his" opinions indicates otherwise. So also does the editorial policy expressed in the first issue of *The Commentator* (February, 1937), a magazine edited by Lowell Thomas and presented as "a medium for the men—and women —who have won wide audiences through the microphone to write what they think without censorship or restrictions of any kind, save space. *The Commentator* will be freer than the air. . . ." It is interesting that the commentators whose radio performances are financed by advertisers should have declared that their magazine would accept no advertising.

Mr. Thomas' radio comments are sponsored by the Sun Oil Company. J. Howard Pew, president of Sun Oil, was a generous contributor to The Crusaders, American Liberty League, Sentinels of the Republic, American Taxpayers' League, and American Federation of Utility Investors. In the August, 1936, issue of Hearst's *Pictorial Review,* Kay Swift reported the following conversation with Mr. Thomas:

"When I asked him about the enormous influence of commentators and what he thought should be done with it, he replied simply, 'I try never to think about it at all.' "

This lack of concern for his effect on the public may be responsible for such slight errors, and such biased reporting, as Mr. Thomas' review of the Child Labor Amendment. In his most persuasive voice he told the audience:

"Of course it is plain that what the opponents of this Child Labor Amendment don't like is that it stretches the long arm of Uncle Sam into the home, to tell parents what they may do with their children. Nobody would care to admit he is in favor of youngsters doing their eight or ten shifts in factories, but if the Child Labor law was made as sweeping as the prohibition law, it would mean that you couldn't even employ little Nellie from next door to come in and wash dishes for 50¢ or come around afternoons and mind the baby while mother plays bridge. Also you couldn't help fourteen year old Joe from across the street work his way through high school by giving him a job tending furnace and mowing the lawn. That seems to be why no fewer than 11 states have gone against this amendment. It needs only two more to defeat it hopelessly."

As the *New Republic* (March 27, 1935)

pointed out, Mr. Thomas was wrong about the measure being hopelessly defeated if two more states voted against it, since it could again be offered for ratification. But even if Mr. Thomas made this mistake because of his ignorance of legislative procedure, his repetition of the propaganda about little Nellie and Joe, which opponents of the Child Labor Amendment tried so hard to popularize, still remains difficult to justify. Except for the comments in the *New Republic,* there appear to be no other critics who objected to the tenor of Mr. Thomas' remarks. Certainly the radio audience did not find anything amiss, for it is accustomed to getting its opinions from the Hearst reporter, Edwin C. Hill, who broadcast the Human Side of the News under the sponsorship of Remington Rand in 1935-36 and of Real Silk Hosiery in 1936-37 and from Gabriel Heatter whose pay checks in 1936-37 came from the Modern Industrial Bank.

Unlike the newspaper writer whose accuracy or lack of it is recorded in printed form, the news broadcaster leaves no public record behind. Anyone can get back issues of newspapers but it requires a special visé to see copies of the radio news scripts. When Remington Rand was sponsoring the March of Time all copies of the scripts were, in fact, destroyed at the completion of the program with the exception of one which was deposited in the safe of its advertising agency, Batten, Barton, Durstine & Osborn. The thought behind this little ceremony, according to Hy Kravif who described it in the *American Spectator,* was that if the scripts were left lying around somebody might steal the idea.

As in the movie world, any program that is successful on the radio is immediately copied. Originality is not desired by Big Business which foots the broadcasting bill; it much prefers something that has been tested and found good. Destroying the scripts of the March of Time has not prevented a dozen or more imitations. To these dramatizations of the news, as to the commentators, the newspaper publishers never vigorously objected. That both types of programs permit and encourage the coloring of news does not seem to trouble the gentlemen who have so valiantly declared that the newspaper publishers must uphold the American heritage of freedom of speech and press. Such programs, it can readily be seen, are not in direct competition with the primary service that newspapers have to offer.

Until the depression, the publishers did not speak harshly of any of the policies of the broadcasting companies. The popular interest in radio was aided and abetted by the publication of station publicity, and of complete radio programs including the names of the advertisers. Things ran along thus happily until the 1930's, when the business departments discovered that they had stood idly by while the editorial departments had been nurturing a little viper. For when the depression laid its heavy hand on advertising appropriations, business cut its allowances for newspaper advertising and increased its outlay for radio. Radio was cheaper, and even though the tremendous coverage guaranteed by the stations had to be bought sight unseen, radio still seemed worth trying. While the business managers of the newspapers watched income shrink, they were goaded into fury by the tremendous gains reported by the broadcasting companies.[3]

[3] According to statistics compiled by the National Broadcasting Company from their own records, those of the American

ANNUAL EXPENDITURES OF ALL NATIONAL ADVERTISERS, BY MEDIUMS

Year	National Newspaper Advertising	Year to Year Ratio (1928=100)	National Magazine Advertising	Year to Year Ratio (1928=100)
1928	$230,000,000	100	$185,204,588	100
1929	260,000,000	113	203,776,077	110
1930	230,000,000	100	201,854,510	109
1931	205,000,000	89	166,555,864	89
1932	160,000,000	70	115,342,606	62
1933	145,000,000	63	93,987,970	51
1934	163,000,000	71	113,514,672	61
1935	167,000,000	73	119,127,613	64

Year	Radio Network Advertising	Year to Year Ratio (1928=100)	Total National Advertising	Year to Year Ratio (1928=100)
1928	$10,252,497	100	$425,457,085	100
1929	18,729,571	182	482,505,648	114
1930	26,815,746	261	458,670,256	108
1931	35,791,999	348	357,347,863	84
1932	39,106,776	381	314,449,382	74
1933	31,516,298	307	270,504,268	64
1934	42,659,461	416	319,174,133	75
1935	48,786,735	476	334,914,348	79

In 1935, the networks' bill of $48,786,735 represented 14.5 cents of every dollar spent for advertising and the $86,492,653 net income of the entire radio industry, including chains and other stations, accounted for 25.8 cents of the advertising dollar. For 1936, radio's estimated income is in excess of $100,000,000. Despite the fact that advertising expenditures for other media also increased, radio was taking a bigger share of the advertising dollar than it had ever claimed before.

Newspaper Publishers Association and the Publishers Information Bureau, the total expenditures of National advertisers for network advertising (exclusive of "talent") increased by 476 percent between the years 1928–35.

The editorial departments did not feel much happier over the state of affairs because the news broadcasters were regularly pirating their program material from the daily newspapers. Compared to 1936, there were comparatively few news broadcasts; but there were enough so that the radio audience could "keep up with the times" and save the cost of a paper.

By 1931, the publishers had had just about enough of it. Some of them announced that they would be good and damned if they would continue to print radio programs free of charge. Theaters paid for advertising, churches paid for advertising, why should the radio stations get it free? But the publishers had stymied themselves. The stations refused to pay—the public was accustomed to finding radio programs in the papers and insisted on getting them. The newspapers finally compromised by printing the programs but omitting the names of the sponsors.

The Lindbergh case and the presidential election of 1932 showed the publishers that they would have to use drastic methods to weaken their rival. Although the Lindbergh kidnapping gave a tremendous boost to newspaper circula-

ANNUAL EXPENDITURES
OF ALL NATIONAL ADVERTISERS

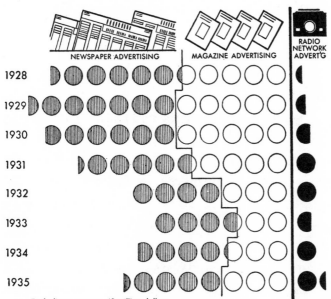

Each disc represents 40 million dollars

NOTE: Advertising on the major networks most clearly approximates advertising in national magazines and in newspapers. But in addition to the money spent for national programs, national advertisers were also buying time from individual stations for "spot advertising." Although the majority of the stations which obtained this additional revenue are members of the chains, the income for spot advertising is not included in the charted total.

tion, the radio stations supplied all of the news to a good part of the public which otherwise would have had to pay for it. They also broadcast the news before the newspapers could get it onto the street, even in special editions. In broadcasting the Hoover-Roosevelt election returns they proved again that radio is faster than the press.

Special arrangements had been made by the press to supply radio stations with the election results. The publishers now realized that such coöperation would never do. They therefore decreed that if radio stations wished to broadcast news, they would have to gather it themselves. This was another tactical error. For the business men who operate radio stations discovered that it is easy, and cheap enough, to hire crack newspaper men. Secondly, and following logically from the first, the station operators decided that since news was costing real money, the sale of news broadcasts should be pushed. Some particularly keen sponsors had already recognized that the sale of soap, gasoline, cosmetics, food, and other products can be increased by entertaining the public with news and gossip. Now the stations' salesmen began an aggressive campaign to merchandise this type of program.

Everyone was well satisfied except the publishers, and at the famous Biltmore Conference they attempted to undo the damage worked by their decree of a few months before. Instead of threatening legal action if radio stations used the news collected by the papers, the publishers offered to supply this news to them through a special Press-Radio Bureau. The stations were to be charged only the administrative and transmission costs of the Bureau. For this coöperation, the stations were to show their good will by discontinuing their own news agencies, broadcasting no news except the thirty-word items supplied by the Bureau (which could not be sold to a "sponsor") and by restricting sponsored newsmen to "interpretation" and "comment." When the Columbia Broadcasting System, as well as the National Broadcasting Company, agreed, the publishers sat around looking as though they had just swallowed the canary.

As a matter of fact the publishers had got the birdie. Of the hundreds of stations which carry network programs, only the few owned by the networks were bound by the Bureau agreement. The others bought news of the Transradio Press Service, an organization started by one of the men who had helped to build Columbia's own press service, or of similar gathering agencies. News so bought or gathered was, of course, offered for sale to advertisers. Because of the exception for commentators and interpreters of the news, the stations owned by the chains did not fare badly either.

The next peace negotiations took place in the spring of 1935 when Mr. William Randolph Hearst's two news-gathering agencies, the International (what can he be thinking of to keep this name?) News Service and the Universal Service, along with the United Press, offered to serve all and any radio stations which would buy their wares. The Associated Press also was willing to make arrangements for the radio industry to secure the advantage of their service. This was good business, because furnishing news for broadcasting has become highly profitable. It has been estimated that for 1936, the agencies serving up news for radio consumption collected $3,000,000. From the sale of this news to sponsors and the time on the air bought for news programs, the radio stations derived an estimated income in excess of $15,000,000. Station WOR, whose management felt that reference to Rockefeller, Morgan and Ford might be disapproved by their advertisers, led all stations for the year in the number of hours devoted to news broadcasting.

The publishers have not been reconciled by the profits derived from the sale of news for broadcasting. Neither are they pleased that the press has become second to the radio in the control of public opinion. The development of facsimile devices by means of which radio receiving sets will be transformed into miniature printing presses, and radio stations enabled to supply the public with news in printed form, further dismays the publishers.

What to do? The more enterprising have already gone into the broadcasting business; others are following. By 1937, according to the statistics of the National Association of Broadcasters, publishers had been licensed to operate or construct 194 stations. In the calendar year 1936, the FCC had issued licenses to 52 publishers and another 102 applications of publishers were pending. Of the ten new stations authorized by the Commission in the first six weeks of 1937, five were grants to publishers. The trend is unmistakable.

Publishers who once expatiated so eloquently on the cause of the free press are now unperturbed by the effect of their operation of radio stations on real freedom of the news. So long as radio and press were separately operated, one served as a check on the other. A vivid example of this was the campaign carried on by the *Knoxville (Tenn.) Journal* during the press-radio war. Whenever the *Journal* considered that a broadcast news bulletin had erred in accuracy, the mistake was pointed out in the following edition of the paper. Other newspapers have similarly checked the accuracy of the broadcasters.

But the competition between the press and the broadcasting industry served a more important purpose. News that a radio station might refuse to broadcast the press would be glad to print, and vice versa. The real guarantee of the free dissemination of news was in this competition.

Now the publishers are attempting to monopolize both radio and press. The danger in this unification of control is illustrated by one of the incidents reported in the Civil Liberties Union study. In July, 1934, State Senator Paul Stewart was campaigning for election to the Oklahoma Corporation Commission. For one of his stump speeches he bought time from WKY, a station owned by a subsidiary of the Oklahoma Publishing Company. When Stewart submitted his speech and the station censors discovered that he intended to attack the publishing company, he was immediately informed that he would have to delete his critical remarks. On his refusal to comply, the station refunded the money which had been paid for the broadcast. The remarks to which the station objected were:

"The Oklahoma Publishing Company, a foreign corporation which owns WKY, the *Oklahoma Farmer-Stockman*, the *Daily Oklahoman*, the *Times* and the *Mistletoe Express* have exposed me through their newspapers and in their editorials. A few years ago the Federal Trade Commission made the utilities go out of the newspaper business and it is my humble judgment that the Oklahoma legislature and the state corporation commission should make the newspapers go out of the utility business. I pledge an earnest effort to that end."

In a speech before the 1935 Institute for Education by Radio, William Hard declared that "the key to the perpetuation of our free institutions . . . is the enhancement of competition. I conclude accordingly that the tendency toward newspaper ownership of radio stations should be legislatively checked."

Not until the 1937 Congressional session did it appear that the legislators finally intended to make such an effort. Representative Otha D. Wearin of Iowa introduced a bill to amend the Communications Act by a provision that:

"It is hereby declared to be against public interest to permit the creation or the continuance of monopolies in the distribution of general information, news, and editorial comment thereon, through any combination resulting in unified control of newspapers, magazines or other printed publications, with radio broadcasting, and after the effective date of this Act it shall be unlawful for any licensee, to any extent, directly or indirectly, in its own person or through an agent, holding corporation, affiliated corporation, by stock ownership in a corporation, or otherwise, (1) to be owned, partially owned, managed or controlled by any person who owns, partially owns, manages, controls, directs, or publishes any newspaper, magazine, or other printed publication circulated or distributed to any extent within the area or zone served by the broadcasting station allotted to such licensee—"

Under the Wearin bill, the publishers' monopoly of broadcasting would be ended by the simple device of prohibiting the renewal of their broadcasting licenses. In the Senate, Burton K. Wheeler was also expected to introduce legislation prohibiting the ownership of radio stations by publishers. Several months before the 1937 Congress opened, Senator Wheeler requested an opinion from Hampson Gary, general counsel of the FCC on the constitutionality of such a regulatory measure. He was informed: "that all radio broadcasting is within the regulatory power of Congress under the commerce clause of the constitution and the power to regulate includes the power to prohibit . . . the owning or controlling of a broadcast station as a business has nothing to do with the freedom of speech or of the press as such . . ."

According to the gossip network, Commissioner Norman Case has vigorously opposed the stampede of the publishers into the radio world. It is his contention that no newspaper should be given more than one radio outlet in its circulation area. But the Commission as a whole has displayed little agitation over the efforts of the publishers to dominate broadcasting.

Their approval of the wholesale purchasing of broadcasting stations by William Randolph Hearst is an indication of the 1936 interpretation of the clause in the Commission Act providing that licenses are to be issued to those who operate "in the public interest, convenience or necessity." All those stories about Mr. Hearst's jingoism were apparently passed over by the commissioners as the ranting of disgruntled muckrakers. Within the space of a few months, the FCC permitted the publisher to increase his radio chain from six to ten and during the same period it granted him permission to increase the transmitting power of two of his stations, in one instance over the examiner's adverse recommendation. Mr. Hearst now owns WINS-New York, WCAE-Pittsburgh, WBAL-Baltimore, WISN-Milwaukee, KYA-San Francisco, KEHE-Los Angeles, and the four new stations: WACO-Waco, KOMA-Oklahoma

City, KNOW-Austin, and KTSA-San Antonio. There are rumors, too, that he is playing the angel to other stations. *Variety* (June 30, 1936) reports that "Hearst is furnishing the backing" for WSAY of Rochester, which is associated with his New York chain. In addition, he has special arrangements with other stations, such as WNEX of Boston, to give wide publicity to the features of the Hearst newspapers.

Through the sale of news to radio stations by his International News Service and Universal Service, he has also broadened his sphere of influence. John Shepard, 3rd, the department-store owner who controls the Yankee and Colonial networks, is one of Mr. Hearst's best customers. Including the stations of these two networks, those in Mr. Hearst's own chain, and the other customers of his news services, there were, in 1936, one hundred and eighty-five stations broadcasting Hearst news to the nation.

Washington is a town of gossipers, and the Commission is one of the most fertile sources of rumors. The approval of the Hearst purchases, and the employment of President Roosevelt's second oldest son, Elliot, as vice president of

Hearst Radio, provided ample opportunity for surmise. Mr. Roosevelt's name appeared on the application for the transfers of the southwestern stations to Mr. Hearst.

When transfer of only two of the four new Hearst stations had been approved, Emile J. Gough, vice president of Hearst Radio, Inc., appeared at a general hearing called by the FCC and declaimed:

"In the allocation of facilities for the dissemination of news, whether by broadcasting, facsimile, television or whatnot, we believe that care should be exercised to the end that those persons and organizations which are experienced in this business, know what is news and what is news service to the public, and who are prepared to develop this service, should be given real consideration.

"Further, we believe that care should be exercised by the Commission in the administration of its regulatory powers to see that news services are not prostituted to any other purpose."

Mr. Hearst is reported to desire a radio station in every city in which there is a Hearst newspaper. Scripps-Howard is also desirous of building a radio chain to match its newspaper holdings.

Shortly before the 1936 presidential election, two applications for new stations were submitted to the Communications Commission by the Scripps-Howard broadcasting subsidiary, the Continental Broadcasting Company. Continental was then operating two stations, WNOX of Knoxville, and WCPO of Cincinnati, but the Commission found that the company's financial condition did not warrant the granting of the two new licenses. According to rumor, it was the awkward handling of the applications by the Scripps-Howard ambassadors in Washington which led to the adverse ruling.

Despite this official rebuff, Scripps-Howard soon arranged to increase its chain. It bought the *Memphis Commercial Appeal,* and with it acquired stations WMC and WNBR. By this purchase, Scripps-Howard became the owner of two of the three biggest stations in Memphis. It also controls the evening paper, the *Memphis News Scimitar,* as well as the morning *Commercial Appeal.*

One of the perils to freedom of the press which has been pointed out frequently in recent years is the diminishing competition in the newspaper world, the buying up of competitors and the growing tendency to monopoly of the news sources. Now we have these same chains buying their way into broadcasting. In sunny California, there are eight broadcasting stations owned by newspapers; two are Mr. Hearst's; four are owned by the McClatchy interests which publish the *Sacramento Bee,* and the *Fresno Bee.* The stations of these two publishing firms have been linked as a network. In Kansas, the Capper publications have two stations; in New York State the Gannett chain has five and a sixth in Connecticut; in Pennsylvania the Steinman brothers have four stations and two more across the state border in Wilmington, Delaware.

The publishers obviously do not see the danger to a free press in the control of newspapers by giant chains. Obviously, then, they cannot see the perils in permitting these chains to acquire chains of broadcasting stations. But the threat to free speech and a free press is apparent to everyone else.

XIII

SOLUTIONS?

THERE is no easy solution for the problems created by the radio. They represent in highly concentrated form the social and economic dilemma of America.

Here we have the vested interests firmly intrenched; here we see business for private profit in full flower.

Banker control is not unique to radio. We have it in every big business. But the financial structure that we have come to accept for other industries creates special problems when applied to broadcasting. For this business is a trafficking in thoughts and opinions, not in ordinary goods. To permit its operation by a few banker-dominated monopolies represents a threat that cannot be disregarded.

This is the fulcrum of the problem. Freedom of speech is a correlative of democracy and has always been accepted as such. It is remarkable

287

then that its perpetuation should have been entrusted to a few monopolists. It is equally astonishing that with the popular sentiment against trusts, the combines of the radio world should be permitted to continue in control.

Partially, this is a result of the public's ignorance. It does not know who controls the radio, nor does it care. To the average listener radio is still merely a source of entertainment; it has no social significance. Partially, it is the result of inertia and perplexity. Even though many are dissatisfied with the present system, with its pandering to "popular" tastes, and its highly commercialized aspects, they ask what better plan can be evolved. The National Association of Broadcasters, the central pressure group of the industry, has effectively popularized the conclusion that the American system, although not perfect, is better than any other that can be devised.

The peril, it repeats, is in any attempt to change the status quo. Look how the radio is used by Mussolini and Hitler. True, broadcasting in the United States is operated for private profit, but the competitive system means a free market, in this instance, a free market for ideas. Does it? With the monopolists in control, is there a free market? Can men motivated by business expediency and class traditions be entrusted with their present vast power?

The public has become accustomed, and therefore amenable to the dictatorship of business; it should understand the danger implicit in this dictatorship when applied to the radio.

The situation must be considered realistically. In an imperfect world it is absurd to imagine that any single part or industry can be operated perfectly. It is easier to say that the money changers must be driven from the market places than to evict them. Compromises are tactical. Advantages must be balanced against disadvantages, gains against retreats. But there are certain steps in the regulation of broadcasting which should be taken immediately, and on which no compromise is possible.

First of all, the growing domination of the air waves by a few small groups of men must be checked. This step must not be confused nor delayed by any general attack on the present system.

The two major chains are now well established. Even though the federal license conveys no property rights to the air and merely grants the privilege of broadcasting on a certain wave length, the rule of priority has become well established. Let us grant then that, by previous use, the two major networks are entitled to their cleared channels and high transmission power. But this does not mean that additional purchases of stations by the networks should be countenanced.

In 1936 the Communications Commission approved the purchase of Station KNX by the Columbia Broadcasting System, giving as one of its reasons that this would further competition between the two networks on the Pacific coast. If the Commission continues this line of reasoning, the holdings of the chains will increase more rapidly in the next few years than they have in the past decade. For the competitive struggle between the major chains is only beginning. Both the National Broadcasting Company and the Columbia Broadcasting System are intent on being the biggest, and in the race for supremacy each is attempting to outdo the other in the number of its stations. If the race is allowed to continue the two chains may eventually divide between them all the broadcasting channels.

Near parity has now been achieved by the two major networks. Neither will be injured in its pocketbook, nor will business competition between them be decreased if the radio law is amended in such a way that neither chain may purchase additional stations, nor if restrictions are placed on the number of stations which may be affiliated with any one group.

The limitation on the ownership of stations would directly affect the newspaper publishers who are now stampeding into radio. This rule, in fact, should be broad enough to apply to any network operator. Since the air channels are limited, since there will never be enough for everyone, it is impossible to justify the assignment to any person or group of more than one license to operate in a given area.

Unquestionably the lobbyists for the networks would apply pressure if such rulings were promulgated. And if pressure did not produce re-

sults they would cry that the government was
robbing "the widows and orphans." Such bleat-
ing has been effective in the fight of the private
"public" utilities against government control.
The investing public now has a stake in the financial success of the National Broadcasting Company through the ownership of stock in the Radio
Corporation of America. That this stake is a
small one, that the public has no voice in the
management of the company, and that it is really
the bankers who have the most to lose, would of
course not be mentioned. Many radio stations
have already followed the lead of the Radio Corporation, the American Telephone and Telegraph Company, and the electric utilities and are
selling or planning to sell stock to the public.
The scheme is transparent. Once the public has
been "let in," the broadcasting industry will have
a more persuasive argument why nothing should
be done to upset the present system, why everything should be done to enable the stations to
earn profits. The stations will be "owned" by
the "peepul," by the widows and orphans who
always seem to be the most conspicuous investors
in industries under attack. If the Communica-

tions Commission were to require that the public
be given adequate warning of the highly specu-
lative character of the industry, which operates
at the pleasure of the government, and on a short-
term license, subsequent wailing about the
widows and orphans may fall flat.

The high-priced lawyers who advise the major
networks would undoubtedly be called upon to
devise a legal method of avoiding the penalties
of a law limiting the ownership of stations, but
a well-drafted statute, an active group of prose-
cutors and heavy penalties—which might include
the revocation of all licenses held by offenders—
would do much to keep in check any attempts to
circumvent the law.

At present, the Communications Commission
requires disclosure of the holdings of major stockholders in radio stations. This information, although part of the public record, is not known to
the public. Every publication using second class
mailing privileges, as all but a few do, is required
to print lists, at regular intervals, giving the
names of major stockholders and officers. There
is no reason why similar publicity on station
ownership should not be required. Just on the

chance that the program managers should decide
that the radio audience would be bored by such
lists, and schedule them for the early morning
hours when comparatively few are listening in,
the regulation should explicitly provide that information on ownership must be given at a time
when the station's maximum audience is tuned
in. This would be, except in special cases, between the hours of 7–10 P. M. A rule requiring
such public disclosures should be made immediately and need not wait the adoption of any of
the other suggested changes.

Similar information should be required from
all organizations or individuals using the radio
for any purpose other than the ballyhooing of
merchandise. If, for example, The Crusaders
were required to announce the names of the ten
biggest contributors of the week, or month, directly before or after each speech, the power of
this fascist group, or of any lobbyist for the special interests, would be ended.

The chain system now means the wasteful use
of air channels for the duplication of programs.
In many sections of the country the radio audience can hear the same "amateur" programs, the

same clowns, the same encomiums for laxatives and cosmetics by tuning in on any one of several stations. This is certainly not a public necessity and it is not in the public interest. If the Communications Commission were to order that not more than one station whose signals can be heard in any given area may, except on special occasions of national importance, broadcast the same program, it would not only provide greater variety of programs but, more important, it would immediately force the two major chains to decrease their holdings. Monopoly, to a limited extent, would have to bow to the demands of the competitive system. It is true that the major chains would continue their ownership of, and affiliation with, the stations with the best wave lengths, but they would have to make their choice and relinquish some. Remember, please, that we are not offering a complete catharsis; we are trying to cure the patient by a slower method.

Since the chain system has proved financially satisfactory, an order by the Commission limiting the scope of chain operations would not discourage this type of broadcasting, but rather would provide the impetus for the formation of new national and regional chains with key stations located throughout the country. Instead of New York, Chicago and Hollywood being the center of our radio culture, as they are today, there would be a greater incentive to develop local talent and local programs.

The realignment in the radio world might have still another salutary result. At present the telephone company is the chief beneficiary of chain broadcasting. The major networks pay it a fortune every year for wire service. But the new chains might very well assert their independence of the telephone company and transmit programs from station to station by the short waves. This has already been successfully done by some groups. With continual improvement in short wave equipment, there is no reason why wireless transmission should not increase. The Commission would, of course, have to assign short waves for this purpose.

There is a real possibility, however, that in the not very distant future the chain system may become obsolete. With the use of greater transmitting power, single stations will be able to send programs across the country. The cost of equipping and maintaining these stations is prohibitive for all but the financially elect. Furthermore, since a few big stations could effectively carry the message of the advertisers to the nation, there would be little need, and therefore little income, for the stations out in the sticks. The big stations would be in complete control. The many dangers, economic and social, of such a development are apparent, and in the fall of 1936 when the Commission held hearings on the problem of granting applications for increased transmission power, some members of the industry urged the Commission to proceed with the greatest caution. But in no field—and this is especially true of radio—can potential social or economic dangers restrain scientific development.

With the medium itself tending to a more absolute monopoly for the few, it should be clear to all that the present laissez-faire attitude cannot be continued. The alternative invariably suggested to control by the money rulers is control by the government. This is no answer. We now have too much interference by the government's radio authority. There is little to be gained by the exchange of one monopoly for another. Unless all the benefits which are reputedly derived from the competitive system are inapplicable to broadcasting, it would appear that what we need is not less competition but more.

Then we need definite limitation of the radio stations' authority to censor. The American Civil Liberties Union has suggested a practical legislative program for accomplishing this objective by amending the present Communications Act in the following manner:

"(1) require each station as a condition of its license to set aside regular periods 'at desirable times of the day and evening for uncensored discussion on a nonprofit basis of public, social, political and economic problems and for educational purposes.'

"(2) make it mandatory for every station presenting a controversial issue to give a hearing to at least one opposing view. (An advisory committee of 'disinterested, representative citizens' would advise the Commission respecting the allocation and use of time for discussion of public questions and for educational purposes.)

"(3) free stations, though not speakers, from legal liability for remarks on such programs.

"(4) compel stations to keep accurate and public records of all applications for time, indicating which were granted and which refused."

Three bills embodying this program were originally introduced by Representative Byron Scott of California on August 23, 1935. They have not yet been acted upon. A fourth bill, providing for the appointment of a special investigating committee, was also shunted into one of the dark corners. Yet the fourth bill has greater possibilities of legislative success than the other three. For periodic investigation of the radio industry has historical precedents. No major industry has been subjected to more investigation. And in no industry have fewer changes been effected as a result of the findings of the investigators. Instead of merely another investigation or, if you will, together with it, we need a more positive contribution by the government.

At one of the 1936 hearings of the Communications Commission on the allocation of the ultra-high frequencies, representatives of the government requested that a major portion of the new wave lengths be set aside for non-profit, public use. No broadcasting company can now claim a prior right to these wave lengths. The granting of the government's application would in no way interfere with the present rights of the industry nor with its exploitation of the wave lengths in the old broadcast band. Yet the denunciation of the government's proposal was extremely bitter. Representative leaders of the industry saw grave dangers in permitting the government to gain a foothold in the broadcasting world.

They want no competition from the government. They want no move made which will jeopardize the maintenance of the status quo. Their arguments, of course, merely beclouded the issue. Men who know all too well that the government through its licensing authority exercises a positive control over the entire industry, piously argued that the freedom of the air from government interference must be continued. They said, and the tears fairly dripped from their words, that to grant the government's request would be the first step toward a government monopoly of broadcasting.

Certainly, said the protagonists of commercialized broadcasting, the government cannot complain of the generosity of the stations in donating the use of their facilities. This is the relationship which the industry wishes to maintain, to operate broadcasting as a profit-making public utility, the government to be the "chiseler" asking for free time. The attitude of the industry is concisely stated in the headline of an article which appeared in *Broadcasting,* the organ of the National Association of Broadcasters. "Uncle Sam on the Air—with Donated Time," it read.

With new wave lengths available for broadcasting, there is every reason why adequate provision should be made for a chain of stations operated by the government. To establish for radio a yardstick comparable to the TVA, to have government and privately operated stations broadcasting side by side, is a compromise with many advantages.

Obviously the government stations must be operated by an unbiased non-political authority (entirely independent of the Communications Commission) and function under an act which explicitly requires that the publicly owned broadcasting facilities provide a public forum where speakers are free from every form of censorship and only personally liable under the well-defined laws of slander and libel.

During the campaign periods, the facilities of

such stations would be available free of charge to all candidates, the time allotted to each determined by a special committee representing all recognized parties. There would be no censorship of such speeches. Candidates who wished additional time on the air would, of course, continue to buy it from the private companies. Aside from the election periods, the government stations would be used by the people's elected representatives to report to their constituents on legislative matters. Since the establishment of a national chain is contemplated, the legislators of each state as well as those who sit in Washington would have ample opportunity to report to the people they represent. Provision would also be made so that the stations could be used by city and town officials. The primary use of the government stations would be to keep the electorate informed on public affairs.

In addition to political discussions, free in every sense of the word, the government stations would be available for debates and analyses of social and economic problems. Minority points of view, as well as those of the majority, would be heard. The stations would also be used by the

educators of the public school system for conducting real schools of the air for adults as well
as for children. Such programs would be broadcast
at desirable hours, not, as they are so frequently
by the commercial broadcasters, at odd times
during the day. With adequate facilities available, and opportunity for perfecting the technique of teaching over the air, the educational
programs in themselves might justify the operation of government stations. As this book goes
to press, the Office of Education, the Department
of the Interior, has inaugurated a new program
over the Columbia network. "Let Freedom
Ring" is the title, and the time of broadcasting
is 10:30 Eastern Standard Time on Monday
evenings. For fast pacing, dramatic presentation
and acting, this program, which is a history of
the fight for civil liberties, has few equals on the
air. The Columbia Broadcasting System is to
be congratulated for transmitting it and the government's impresarios for proving that they can
put on a show immeasurably better than the majority used to ballyhoo business.

These stations, of course, would continue many
of the popular government programs now broad-

cast by the major chains as one of their public services. The Farm and Home Hour, arranged by the Department of Agriculture and the NBC, is so popular that, according to one of the commentators in the trade, "Millions would rather go without lunch than miss its varied attractions." Other government bureaus might easily develop similarly popular programs. With the present interest in consumer activities the bureaus working directly in this field should command much attention. By naming names of companies against which the food and drug authorities have taken action, the hundred million guinea pigs would be supplied with accurate news. Some of the advertisers who pay high prices to the privately operated stations to ballyhoo their products would undoubtedly resent the government's "muckraking." But since the publicly owned stations would broadcast no advertising, and would be independent of the advertisers, service to the public and not business expediency would be the determining factor.

Essentially, the government stations would not compete in supplying song and dance acts, although if the WPA and similar federal projects are continued, there is no reason why they should not provide dramatic and musical programs. Considering the highly commercialized entertainment now offered for children, the government's playwrights and actors might be immediately called upon to offer substitutes for the commercialized horror hours. The WPA theater might also perform its plays for the unseen adult audience. Radio work would not be new for the WPA. Many of its programs have already been broadcast by the commercial radio stations as a "public service." Federal Music Project No. 1 has also made recordings of its one-hundred-piece string orchestra directed by Nickolai Sokoloff for small stations serving areas where government orchestras have not been established. Obviously, the programs of the government station can be varied and vital. They would, of course, compete for an audience with the commercial stations and they would have to put on interesting performances to hold their public. By the same token, the commercial broadcasters would have a new competitor which would be in a unique position to show how broadcasting can serve the public interest. The public needs such a yardstick to take the measure of the American system; the industry itself should welcome it as proof that the present broadcasting-for-profit system operates for the common good.

How is the money for the operation of publicly owned stations to be obtained? Paradoxically, the commercial stations might be called upon to provide part of the funds required. There has been frequent discussion whether broadcasting licenses should be issued free and, except for precedent, there appears to be no reason why the free grants should be continued. Like the motorist who pays in his license fee for the privilege of using the public roads, the owner of a broadcasting station might also pay a fee for using the public's air channels. The fee might, for example, be fixed according to transmitting power, just as the motor laws of some states provide a charge scale for auto licenses according to the weight of the vehicle.

When the appropriation for the fiscal year 1937–1938 was being considered by the House Appropriation Committee, Representative Richard B. Wigglesworth suggested another method of taxing the broadcasting industry. After discussing the industry's $100,000,000 gross income, he turned to Judge Sykes, Chairman of the Commission's Broadcasting division, and asked:

"If you were to charge, say 10 percent of the gross earnings, it would make quite a contribution to the revenue of the government, would it not?"

"Yes," responded Judge Sykes. "We have discussed here several times the question of whether or not the Commission should be self-supporting . . . or at least bring into the government a sufficient amount of money to compensate for what it costs the government."

If some such plan were evolved, if the money now appropriated for the operation of the Commission were no longer needed for that purpose, it could be used for the construction and operation of government-owned stations.

The selection of the personnel of the publicly owned stations would entail greater problems. Everything, of course, would depend on the caliber and the skill of the men chosen. But for the other yardstick agencies, capable men have been found who were eager to render a public service. There is no reason to believe that outstanding men cannot be enlisted for the radio project. It is unnecessary to point out that politics must play no part in the selection of the personnel.

The Federal Radio Commission was originally discredited by the political character of its personnel, and subsequent appointments have by no means disproved the charges that the Commission has been used to solve patronage problems. Its record also shows how a government body may usurp authority when the act under which it operates does not adequately limit its powers. There is no question but that the Commission's dictatorship of the industry must be checked. If we are to have a "free radio" then let's have it. Our legislative draftsmen might well consider whether the Commission's present power to make rules and regulations should be continued. They might also take under advisement whether the Commission should not be forced to discontinue the short-term licensing system. The excuse that this system makes reallocation of the air channels easier is absurd. There have been no significant changes in the assignment of wave lengths since the air channels originally were allotted. The short-term licensing is merely a device through which the Commission can exert pressure. Freeing radio stations from the necessity of applying to the Commission every six months for permission to continue in business would by no means be a license to misbehave. The Commission has the right to revoke licenses. It can be a good enough policeman without the short-term licensing—in fact, if the Commissioners and their staff were freed of the routine work created by the short-term licenses, they might be available for more important policing.

One section of the Communications Act calls for immediate revision. The President is now given the power to take over any, or all, stations upon proclamation "that there exists . . . a threat of war . . . or other national emergency." This is a direct refutation of the constitutional guarantee of free speech. If a dictator wishes to seize the broadcasting facilities, let him do so at his peril. The law should not make such a seizure legal.

About this, and other of radio's problems, we need more free discussion. We need greater realization that radio is not a toy, not a special gift to the advertising profession, but an instrument that can enslave or free. We need a sufficiently aroused public opinion so that radio broadcasting in the United States will in truth be made to serve the public interest, convenience and necessity.